1100 CRAZY FUN & RANDOM FACTS YOU WON'T BELIEVE

THE KNOWLEDGE ENCYCLOPEDIA TO WIN TRIVIA

SCOTT MATTHEWS

7 BENEFITS OF READING FACTS

1. Knowledge
2. Stress Reduction
3. Mental Stimulation
4. Better Writing Skills
5. Vocabulary Expansion
6. Memory Improvement
7. Stronger Analytical Thinking Skills

The more that you read, the more things you will know. The more you learn, the more places you'll go.

— Dr. Seuss

ABOUT THE AUTHOR

 Scott Matthews is a geologist, world traveller and author of the 'Amazing World Facts' series! He was born in Brooklyn New York by immigrant parents from the Ukraine but grew up in North Carolina. Scott studied at Duke University where he graduated with a degree in Geology and History.

His studies allowed him to travel the globe where he saw and learned amazing trivial knowledge with his many encounters. With the vast amount of interesting information he accumulated he created his best selling books 'Random, Interesting & Fun Facts You Need To Know'.

He hopes these facts will provide you with hours of fun, knowledge, entertainment and laughter.

If you gain any knowledge from this book, think it's fun and could put a smile on someone's face, he would greatly appreciate your review on Amazon.

1100 FACTS

1. Psychopaths don't have the ability to see the negative consequences of their actions, only the positive ones.

2. Women named Isabella get a free lifetime admission to the "Isabella Stewart Gardner Museum" in Boston.

3. Nicholas Cage once woke up at home in the middle of the night and found an almost naked man wearing only a leather jacket eating a fudgesicle in front of his bed. After that, the actor could no longer live in that house and later moved to the Bahamas.

4. McDonald's has Happy Meal boxes in some locations in Sweden that can fold into virtual reality viewers that are called Happy Goggles.

5. Female spotted hyenas don't actually have a vagina, but a type of pseudo-penis. They are significantly larger than their male counterparts and are the more dominant ones of the species.

6. Based on reports done by the World Health Organization, in the last forty five years, suicide rates have increased by 60% worldwide. In fact, the approximate mortality rate is sixteen per 100,000 people, or one death every forty seconds.

7. Guolizhuang is an exotic restaurant in Beijing; its menu consists almost entirely of penis and testicle dishes.

8. As of 2012, in Italy it's illegal to tell a man that he has no balls, since it hurts male pride.

9. In the United States, the first drug law was to forbid Chinese opium dens.

10. Colombian drug lord Pablo Escobar got to build his own prison in 1991 known as La Cathedral. It had a soccer field, a giant dollhouse, a bar, a Jacuzzi, and even a waterfall. He stayed there for only one year and one month after he was caught torturing his guests. After that he was back on the run.

11. In 2013, a study conducted by researchers at The Harvard School of Public Health revealed that drinking several cups of coffee a day could reduce the risk of suicide in men and women by about 50%.

12. On September 13, 1916, an elephant nicknamed Murderous Mary was hung in the town of Erwin, Tennessee, because she mauled one of her keepers to death. To do so, a huge crane was required. At the time, hanging and lynching were both a popular form of justice.

13. In order to taunt police, a convicted pedophile named Christopher Paul Neil posted a picture of himself with a swirl effect on his face. The image, however, was unswirled by Interpol revealing his face, and he was arrested.

14. Scaphism was a horrifying ancient type of torturous execution. People killed using this method were made to drink very high amounts of honey and milk, and were then stripped naked, and placed between two hollow trunks, or rowboats. Some more honey would be put on the person's body, and that would attract all sorts of vermin and insects, which would burrow into the person's body and eat him from the inside out, leaving them to die a horrible death.

15. Crystal meth used to be prescribed as a diet aid after the Second World War; it actually remained legal right up until the 1970's.

16. Cecil Chao, a Hong Kong billionaire, once offered one hundred and

twenty million dollars to anyone who could turn his lesbian daughter straight.

17. Gun silencers don't actually silence a gun. The hot gases released after a gun is shot expand quickly and create shock waves when they leave the chamber of the gun. Silencers contain a series of expansion chambers that cool and dissipate the gases before they leave the barrel of the gun. They work similarly to the muffler on your car.

18. A survey released by Travelzoo revealed that 64% of Americans confess to peeing in the pool or ocean while on vacation.

19. Red squirrels are able to make their own mushroom jerky. To keep it better over the winter, they hang fungi out to dry between tree branches. Mushroom jerky is less likely to infect their larder with insect larvae and nematodes.

20. In order to attract a partner, the peacock spider does a little mating dance, with each spider having its own unique style of dance.

21. Hugh Clarke, a judge from Michigan, actually held himself in contempt after his own smartphone rang in court.

22. After being born and within the first ten minutes, a duckling will consider anything that it meets as its parent forever.

23. During Hurricane Katrina, hundreds of inmates were left to die in their cells because officials abandoned Orleans Parish Prison.

24. Based on reports issued by the Literacy Project Foundation, forty five million Americans are functionally illiterate and cannot read above a fifth grade level. Moreover, 50% of adults cannot read a book written at an eighth grade level.

25. The fastest aircraft made by man is the SR 71 which flew over four thousand missiles while it was in service.

26. Some metal pieces of the fallen World Trade Center were used to build both of NASA's Mars Rovers. The metal was made into shields to protect drilling mechanisms.

27. Neo, the lead character in the movie "The Matrix," was actually

offered to Will Smith, but he turned it down to do "Wild, Wild West" instead.

28. In 1994, a man named Tony Cicoria was standing next to a public telephone when he was struck by lightning. A nurse, who was waiting there to use the same phone, resuscitated him. Shortly after his recovery, he noticed that his head became flooded with music and decided to get a piano; he is now a successful composer and performer.

29. The pyramids of Giza were more ancient to the ancient Romans than Rome is ancient to us.

30. The largest frog in the world is the Goliath frog. It can reach up to 12.5 inches (thirty one centimeters) in length and weigh seven pounds (three kilograms).

31. In June of 2016, a massive theft of Twitter usernames and passwords took place, affecting almost thirty three million customers. According to the security company LeakedSource, more than 120,000 people had used the password "123456."

32. In 1945, Harold Matson and Elliot Handler started Mattel Toy Company in a garage. The name Mattel is a combination of their names. They actually started out by producing picture frames, but when Elliot started making dollhouse furniture from the picture frames scraps, they were so successful that they switched over to making only toys.

33. Einstein actually had an illegitimate daughter. She was born in 1902.

34. There is a deep-sea squid called the "Strawberry Squid" that has mismatched eyes and looks like a strawberry. It has one large, light-colored eye that is angled upwards; and a smaller, darker eye that is angled downwards. One eye evolved to look for predators while the other evolved to look for prey.

35. Mark Zuckerberg initially claimed publically that there would never be a dislike button as it would be "bad for the world."

36. It has been scientifically proven that taking a warm bath before bed

helps you sleep better. When our bodies cool before rest, melatonin is released, which is the hormone that induces sleep. So heating yourself up before bed will speed up the cooling process and you will feel tired quicker.

37. Li Ka-shing is the richest man in Hong Kong. He dropped out of school before he turned sixteen and now has an estimated net worth of $20.1 billion.

38. Astronaut Buzz Aldrin was requested to fill out a military travel voucher for reimbursement for his mission to the moon; he was actually reimbursed $33.31.

39. "The Glory Hole" is a drain hole with a diameter of seventy two feet (twenty two meters) situated in Napa, California, in the Monticello Dam.

40. Jadarite is a type of mineral that was discovered in a Serbian mine. It has the same chemical composition as Kryptonite, the one described in the Superman movies.

41. A violin that uses three strands of golden silk spun by an Australian golden orb spider has been developed at Imperial College London. To customize different sounds, the composite material of silk fibers and a binding agent can actually be mixed and used to improve or vary the acoustic properties of the instrument.

42. A man named Forest Fenn hid a treasure worth between one and three million dollars in the Rocky Mountains. To find it you have to solve his riddle, which no one has yet done.

43. According to the Guinness Book of World Records, the world's tiniest shark is the dwarf lantern shark; a male measures only about 6.3 inches (sixteen centimeters) in length.

44. The actor Peter Meyhew who played Chewbacca in the Star Wars films had to be escorted by crew members dressed in brightly colored vests while shooting in the forest of the Pacific Northwest, to ensure that he wasn't shot by hunters who would mistake him for Bigfoot.

45. Colonel Sanders used to make surprise visits to KFC restaurants. If

he wasn't happy with the quality of food, he would throw everything on the ground and curse at the employees.

46. Based on information provided by the Center of Disease Control and Prevention, one in six US adults binge drinks about four times a month.

47. In July 2016, after a night of drinking with friends, thirty three year old British man Simon Smith changed his name to Bacon Double Cheeseburger.

48. The jingle "State Farm Like a Good Neighbor" was written by singer Barry Manilow. He was paid only $500 for it.

49. A study from biologists at Newfoundland's University suggested that bread is junk food for ducks as it leads them to becoming overweight and disease-ridden.

50. To make change for a dollar in the US, there are 293 different combinations.

51. "Backrub" was the name originally given to Google.

52. If you want to climb Mount Everest, you have to save between $60,000 and $120,000. This price includes sherpas, supplies, and permits.

53. In 2016, a rare first edition of Philosophiae Naturalis Principia Mathematica by Sir Isaac Newton was sold for $3.7 million.

54. Actor John Ratzenberger, known for his role as Cliff Clavin in the TV hit Cheers, is the only actor who has voiced characters in every single Pixar movie.

55. Jackie Chan is the best paid actor in Asia.

56. The word zip in "zip code" is actually an acronym for Zone Improvement Plan.

57. The average human head weighs ten pounds (4.5 kilograms).

58. The youngest president in US history was Theodore Roosevelt at

just forty two years old. He took office in 1901, after the assassination of William McKinley, for whom he served as vice president.

59. One of the best vasectomy doctors found in Austin, Texas, is named Dick Chop.

60. The Latin word for porcupine literally means "quill pig." There are over two dozen porcupine species known and they all boast a coat of needle like quills. Some of them, like those of Africa's crested porcupine, are nearly a foot (thirty-centimeter) long.

61. In 2016, a survey done by Pew Research concluded that of 1,520 adults living in all fifty American states and the District of Columbia, over one in four people didn't read a single book within the last twelve months.

62. Only 10% of the world's population lives in the southern hemisphere. That means there's only eight hundred million in the south compared to the six billion in the north.

63. The richest superhero to exist is Black Panther who has an estimated net worth of five hundred billion dollars. Bruce Wayne only has a net worth of eighty billion while Tony Stark's estimated net worth was one hundred billion dollars.

64. Bald eagles are able to live for up to fifty years.

65. Daniel Radcliffe celebrated winning his role in Harry Potter by watching an extra episode of Fawlty Towers and staying up half an hour longer than usual.

66. One of the inventors of the taser, John H. Jack Cover, named it after his literary hero Tom Swift. The word is actually an acronym for Thomas A. Swift's Electric Rifle. Cover just added the "A" to Tom Swift's name.

67. The Naviator is a drone that is not only able to fly but also swim. It was developed by Javier Diaz, a professor at the Department of Mechanical and Aerospace Engineering at Rutgers University.

68. Ding Dong is a town located in Bell County, Texas.

69. Male hippopotamuses size each other up by opening their mouths up to 150 degrees and stretching them up to 4.9 feet (1.5 meters) in length.

70. There is a steel and glass structure called "Tilt" on the 94th floor of the John Hancock Center in Chicago, which allows people to hover 1,000 feet (305 meters) over the city. The structure has three overhead hydraulic actuators that rotate the enclosed moving platform and tilts you out thirty degrees over the edge of the building.

71. A group of buffalos is called a gang.

72. Although hummingbirds cannot walk or hop, they are able to shuffle with their extremely short, weak legs.

73. During the Victorian era and the early 20th century, people used to send vinegar Valentine's as well as the usual Valentine's cards on Valentine's Day. Sold in the United States and Britain, the cards featured an illustration and a short verse of insult instead of love. It was a way for people to insult someone without actually doing it to their face.

74. A wine for cats was created by a company called Apollo Peak, in Colorado. It contains no alcohol and is made of catnip with beets to give it the typical red wine color. It comes in flavors like pinot meow and moscato. Single serving bottles cost $5 while eight-ounce bottles cost $12.

75. There is a 229 feet (seventy meter) underground motel room located in a 65,000,000 year old cave at The Grand Canyon Caverns. It is considered the deepest, darkest, oldest, and quietest, motel room in the world.

76. Whittier is a town in Alaska where almost everyone works under the same roof. Inside the fourteen story building there is a school, police station, bed and breakfast, and two convenience stores.

77. In Egypt, every president that has held the position has died in office or been arrested into military custody.

78. Before Hugh Jackman took up the role of Wolverine in X-men, he didn't know that they were an actual animal.

79. There are more trade regulations imposed upon bananas than upon AK-47s.

80. Studies performed by astronomers and geologists led by J. Alexis Rodriguez, at the Planetary Science Institute at Tucson, Arizona, revealed the occurrence of two massive tsunamis on Mars billions of years ago. They were both triggered by meteor impacts, creating waves as high as 150 feet (forty five meters).

81. A study published in the Journal of Behavior Therapy and Experimental Psychiatry revealed that our mood can affect how we walk and vice versa. If we are sad, we walk slumped-shouldered; if we are happy, we walk bouncing. Additionally, if we imitate a happy walk, it makes us feel happier, and sadder if we imitate a sad way of walking.

82. Charles Dickens wrote "A Christmas Carol" in only six weeks. In fact, Tiny Tim and Bob Cratchet helped speed up the process.

83. In South Africa, a group of high school girls from Cape Town have designed and built the first private satellite of the continent. It was launched into space in May of 2017 and it collects information on agriculture and food security within the continent.

84. In 2015, a study published in BMC Evolutionary Biology found that after analyzing the spine shapes of modern humans who suffer from lower back pain, they have spines that are similar to chimpanzees; therefore, they are less well-adapted for walking upright.

85. College student Dave MacPherson was the very first guest to enter Disneyland. He didn't ride a single attraction that time because he had to get back to school. However, he was awarded a life-long ticket to Disneyland with up to three guests. The ticket was later extended to include Disney parks around the world.

86. Only military and government officials can own motor vehicles in North Korea.

87. The title "Mrs." has an "r" in it because the abbreviation comes from mistress, not missus.

88. The world's biggest online shopping day is on Single's Day in China; it's when uncoupled folks celebrate by buying themselves gifts.

89. The University of Chicago did a study that found rats that were trained to press a lever to receive food would stop pressing the button once they found out that another rat would receive an electric shock.

90. In Poland, they don't say "not my problem" and instead say "not my circus, not my monkey."

91. During the First World War, to conceal observation posts on the battleground, soldiers used camouflage trees. Camouflage artists sketched actual battle damaged trees in the battlefield. They were made behind lines by cutting down a real tree at night and replacing a battle worn tree with the replica. This provided a surveillance point where there was usually a flat exposed area.

92. Peregrine falcons are able to bomb their prey from above at up to 199 miles (320 kilometers) per hour.

93. In 2013, the world's first two-headed sea slug was found by dive master Nash Baiti while on vacation in Borneo. Besides the two heads, it had male and female organs, was bright neon orange and green in color, and toxic.

94. In the 1850's, to avoid people racing in their horse carriages, the pathways of the roads in Central Park were designed to be curved.

95. There is an underground town in Australia where all inhabitants, around 200 people, live in abandoned opal mines. Residents there have electricity and plumbing facilities, and it's known that they find great quantities of opal when renovating.

96. The Vikings used to find new lands by releasing ravens from their boats and following where they went. They became their favorite symbol and resulted in them using the bird on their flag.

97. The longest standing alliance in the world is held between the United Kingdom and Portugal, which started in 1386.

98. There is a cereal cafe in London known as The Cereal Killer Café

where you can eat hundreds of different kinds of cereal from around the world.

99. "127 Sale" is known as the world's longest yard sale. It took place between August 4 and August 7 of 2016 and extended over 621 miles (1,000 kilometers) throughout four American states: Covington, Kentucky, Gadsden, and Alabama. People selling goods lined the roadside along the US Highway 127 and the Lookout Mountain Parkway.

100. The female lion does the majority of the hunting. Sporadically, the male will join only when the prey is particularly large, like a buffalo.

101. Coby the Cat is a British cat that has an account on Instagram with over 1.1 million followers.

102. Female kangaroos have three vaginas. Two of them are located on the outside and are for sperm, and lead to two uteruses, while the middle one is for giving birth.

103. Back in 1919, if you bought a single share of Coca Cola stock, it would be $40. If you kept it till today, it would be worth $9.8 million.

104. A few days after the release of "The Marshall Mathers LP 2" album by Eminem, his childhood home that is on the cover strangely caught fire and was left in ruin.

105. In some parts of South Asia, Africa, and China, monkey brains are considered a delicacy and an easily digestible substance. It's often given to children, and there are even entire cookbooks dedicated on how to cook them.

106. In 1930, eleven year old Venetia Burney gave the name to the planet Pluto. She suggested the name Pluto to her grandfather, who in turn suggested it to a friend who happened to be an astronomy professor at Oxford University.

107. According to a scientific study conducted in 2008, owning a cat can help reduce a human being's risk of a heart attack or stroke by over 33%.

108. While director James Cameron was editing the Titanic, he taped a razor blade to the side of the computer with instructions that said: "Use

only if the film sucks." However, the film went on to gross a total of $1.84 billion worldwide.

109. On January 9, 1493, when sailing near the Dominican Republic, three mermaids were supposedly seen in the water by famous Italian explorer Christopher Columbus. He described them as being not half as beautiful as they are painted. The creatures turned out to be manatees.

110. The Nigerian police force once arrested a goat as one of the suspects for attempted armed robbery.

111. In Japan, there is a traditional pastime among children consisting of molding mud balls by hand into perfect spheres, which are later dried, and polished into a shiny luster. The balls are called "hikaru dorodango."

112. A solar plane that is set to become the first ever solar plane to reach the stratosphere was created by Swiss adventurer Raphael Domjan. It's a sleek white two seater with long wings that are covered with 237 square feet (seventy two square meters) of solar panels.

113. The University of Exeter did studies that found that sharks have their own characteristics and personalities. Some sharks are more social while some are reserved and shy.

114. Caterpillars completely turn into liquid in a cocoon, but when becoming a moth or butterfly, they still remember their life as a caterpillar.

115. Dr. Wuzong Zhou of Saint Andrews University discovered that every second that a candle flame burns, approximately 1.5 million diamond nanoparticles are created, which unfortunately are burned away during the process. His findings, however, could lead to research into how diamonds could be created in a less expensive way.

116. The jawbone or mandible is the hardest bone in the human body. It's also the largest and strongest bone in the human face.

117. Chocolate Avenue is a street in Hershey, Pennsylvania. The avenue runs past the original Hershey's Chocolate factory and it has street lights shaped like Hershey Kisses.

118. King Tutankhamun was not buried alone. Two miniature coffins that contained two fetuses were also found in the chamber. Recent DNA analyses suggest that one of the mummies was his stillborn daughter and the other was likely his child also, although experts believe that he left no living heirs.

119. Porphyrophobia is the fear of the color purple.

120. The oldest blogger in the world is 105 year old Swedish woman Dagny Carlsson. She took a course in informatics at ninety nine years old and has been blogging ever since.

121. The first role that actor Brad Pitt played was a chicken. He wore a chicken suit to bring customers to a restaurant called El Pollo Loco in Hollywood. Today the fifty six year old actor has now been in more than seventy movies and won an Academy Award out of five nominations.

122. The lowest graduation rate in Canada is found in Nunavut, in the Northwest Territories, where only 57% of students actually finish high school.

123. In the yearly Yale-Harvard football game of 2004, the students of Yale tricked the Harvard crowd to hold up cards that formed the words "we suck," by telling them it would spell "go Harvard." Yale still ended up losing the game.

124. Martin Luther King Jr. was originally named Michael. When his father traveled to Germany, he became deeply inspired by the protestant reformation leader Martin Luther. In consequence, he changed his own name as well as the name of his five year old son.

125. Elvis Presley had a twin brother who died at birth. His name was Jessie Garon.

126. Bat's wings are actually made up of cartilage with small amounts of calcium. The bones are similar to our fingers, except that they are more flexible.

127. On December 7, 1972, the crew of the Apollo 17 space shuttle took the famous picture of the Earth known as "The Blue Marble," the

only whole Earth photo taken by human hands. Since then, nobody has been able to be far enough from Earth to take a similar photo.

128. Argentina had five presidents during the last week of 2001 and first week of 2002. The string of presidents started when Fernando de La Rua resigned in December of 2001. The last of the five was appointed in January of 2002 during major protests.

129. The island on the TV show "Gilligan's Island" was created in Hollywood, in the middle of an artificial lake in CBS's studios. The set cost $75,000 to build and it had artificial palm trees mixed in with real plants and flowers.

130. The barber's pole colors of red, white, and blue are a legacy of an era when people went to barbers not just to have a haircut or shave, but also for bloodletting and other medical procedures. At that time, barbers used to cut hair, do some bloodletting, pull teeth, and even set broken bones.

131. The only two countries to depict the outline of their nation on their flag are Cypress and Kosovo.

132. On April 18, 1981, the longest professional baseball game took place between the Pawtucket Red Sox and the Rochester Red Wings. It lasted thirty two innings before being stopped to be resumed on June 23 when one more inning was played.

133. Between 1876 and 2013, the number of attacks reported by great white sharks was 280 globally, and only seventy seven have resulted in a fatality. In comparison, deer kill nearly 200 people a year in the US alone.

134. There are only two words in the English language that have all the vowels, including Y, in alphabetical order: facetiously and abstemiously.

135. In 1862, fractional currency comprising ten, twenty-five and fifty cent denominations were issued by the US government in the form of notes. They were printed between August 21, 1862, and May 29, 1863. Today, they are extremely rare and valuable.

136. In October, 2016, in Serbia, a great number of natural snowballs

showed up on a beach. They spanned ten miles (seventeen kilometers) and ranged in size from tennis balls to being up to almost one meter wide. It was an unusual phenomenon where pieces of ice were formed and then rolled by wind and water until they became snowballs.

137. The Suriname toad has holes in her back that are used to give birth. They develop eggs embedded in their backs and eventually they hatch and crawl out of the holes.

138. Michael Buffer, a ring announcer, has trademarked the term "Let's get ready to…" which has netted him over four hundred million dollars.

139. In January of 2017, in the Hunan province in southwestern China, an international team of scientists from the United States, France, and China discovered a new species of prehistoric otter that is 6.24 million years old. It was named the siamogale melilutra; it was about the size of a wolf, and weighed around 110 pounds (fifty kilograms). That is almost twice as large as the largest living otter.

140. The opossum is actually immune to bee stings, scorpion stings, rattlesnake venom, and toxins like botulism.

141. The speed of light in a vacuum can travel 186,282 miles (299,727 kilometers) per second.

142. White supremacist and racist Craig Cobb agreed to take a genetic test and received the results live on television. Surprisingly for him, he was found to be 14% Sub-Saharan African.

143. During the 1500's and 1600's, women who were seen gossiping, riotous, or troublesome were made to wear the scold's bridle, also known as branks, as punishment. It was made of an iron frame that encased the head, and at the front was a bridle or bit, like a horse, that extended into the mouth and held down the tongue with a spiked plate. It literally made it impossible to speak, and was basically a muzzle for a woman.

144. Lions and jaguars react to catnip similarly to domestic cats, by sniffing, licking and rubbing their chins and bodies on the item that it was sprayed on.

145. The term used to call a group of bears is a sloth of bears.

146. Based on reports by the National Oceanic and Atmospheric Administration and NASA, the hottest month in 136 years of record keeping was July 2016.

147. Breast bags were the name given to bras in medieval times.

148. Rhinestones got their name from the Rhine River. In fact, the Austrian factory that produced them used energy that was driven by the Rhine River.

149. The pill bugs, aka "roly poly bugs," are actually crustaceans. They are related to shrimp and crayfish, they breathe with gills and need humidity and moisture to survive.

150. There is a correlation between childhood defiance and success later on in life, as concluded by a forty year long study published in Developmental Psychology.

151. Dyslexic people actually see numbers and letters backwards. It's basically a reading disorder, not a vision or seeing disorder. This means that Braille readers can also be dyslexic.

152. An underpass intended for the blue feathered korora penguins was built in the south island town of Oamaru, in New Zealand, so that they can get to their nesting sites every night.

153. Dwayne "The Rock" Johnson created a motivational alarm clock app that helps you get out of bed and meet your personal goals. There are twenty five ringtones to choose from that were created by The Rock himself and it has no snooze button. Among the ringtones there's one, for example, that is just a mash up of sounds that come from his dog, a couple where he just keeps repeating the words beep and ring-ring, and another where he smashes a harp.

154. It was illegal to show your face in Chicago if you were ugly before 1974.

155. When cats bring back home a dead animal, they are actually showing its owners how to catch and eat prey, just like they would teach

their young in the wild. This is due to their natural role as a mother and teacher.

156. During Roman times, salt used to be highly precious. It was worth its weight in gold and soldiers were sometimes paid in salt, hence the word salary.

157. The queen cow of milk production was won by Robert Behnke, a Wisconsin dairy farmer. His cow, Gigi, has produced more milk in one year than any other cow with 8,700 gallons (32,933 liters); three times the national average for a dairy cow to produce in a year.

158. In December of 2016, Wisdom, the albatross known as the oldest breeding wild bird, laid an egg at the ripe old age of sixty-six, at the Midway Atoll National Wildlife Refuge in Hawaii.

159. The largest feet in the NBA go to Bob Lanier and Shaquille O'neal. They both have size twenty two feet. Bob Lanier has a height of 6 foot 8 (2.08 meters) while Shaq is seven foot (2.13 meters).

160. In 1883, one year after the Brooklyn Bridge opened, twenty-one elephants were led by circus performer P. T. Barnum across it as a way to prove the bridge's strength.

161. The rings of planet Saturn are made up of dust, rock, and ice accumulated from passing comets and meteorite impacts on Saturn's moons.

162. Loving someone and being loved in return makes wounds heal faster, as different research conducted at the University of North Carolina have shown. This is due to the release of oxytocin in the blood.

163. The word "SIM" in SIM card stands for Subscriber Identification Module.

164. The guitarist from the band Queen, Brian May, actually has a PhD in astrophysics. He put aside his academic pursuits for three decades to become a rock star; in 2007 he returned to school to complete and receive his degree.

165. The average a musician makes for every thousand dollars worth of sales in the industry is roughly twenty three dollars.

166. According to a study performed by researchers at the University of Bristol, bees leave a scent on surfaces with their feet. The bees are able to detect the smell and distinguish if it is their own scent, a relative's, or a stranger's.

167. In 2002, an entire family was saved by actor Vin Diesel from a burning car accident.

168. Up to 4% of the sand on the beaches of Normandy today are made of shrapnel from the D-Day fight that took place in 1944.

169. In March of 2017, the iconic rock formation known as the Azure Window, a tourist attraction in Malta, collapsed into the sea after being there for thousands of years.

170. Llamas and alpacas are able to interbreed successfully. Their offspring is called "huarizo."

171. Samuel L. Jackson used to be Bill Cosby's camera stand-in on "The Cosby Show" before he became a movie star.

172. In 2015, a teenager often broke into homes in Colorado to steal snacks, specifically Hot Pockets, and to watch Netflix. No cash or other valuables were ever stolen, only snacks and Netflix.

173. Sanduk Ruit, who is a doctor in Nepal, has restored the vision of over one hundred thousand people in the developing world.

174. Although wearing a wooden prosthetic leg, gymnast George Eiser won three gold medals, two silver, and a bronze in the 1904 Summer Olympics.

175. When horror movies make us jump of fright, our bodies react by going into flight or fight mode because of the connections our brains make between the fake events on the screen and the real events we have actually experienced or even just been told about.

176. As a substitute to seeing eye dogs, there are miniature guide horses

that the blind can use. Some of the advantages include an average life-span of thirty years and a 350-degree vision.

177. The seaside resort of San Alfonso del Mar, in Chile, houses the largest pool of the world. It was built in 2006 and is 114 feet (thirty five meters) deep. Around sixty six million gallons (249 million liters) of water is needed to fill it in.

178. The Crooked Forest, in Northwest Poland, is a forest of about 400 pine trees that grow with a ninety degree bend at the base of their trunks before rising vertically again.

179. In Pune, India, there is a school that encourages students to preserve water by pouring leftover drinking water from their bottles into a large tank before they go home every day. The water is then used for watering plants and trees or for other non-drinking purposes.

180. There is an uninhibited granite islet named Rockall in the Atlantic ocean where less than twenty people have been to. That means that more people have stepped foot on the moon than have been to Rockall.

181. Thanks to his role in mediating the Treaty of Portsmouth, which ended the Russo-Japanese War, Theodore Roosevelt won the Nobel Peace Prize in 1906, becoming the first American to get the award. He later used the prize money to fund a trust to promote industrial peace.

182. The seventh largest human gathering in the history of the world occurred in the city of Chicago, where it was estimated that five million people gathered at Grant Park for a rally to celebrate the Cubs World Series win.

183. Based on reports provided by National Geographic, there used to be around 100,000 wild tigers in Asia a century ago. Unfortunately, due to poaching, there are only about 3,200 today.

184. Tony Fernandez, the CEO of Air Asia, once made a bet with Sir Richard Branson on who would be the winner of the 2010 Grand Prix in Abu Dhabi. Richard lost and had to work as a female flight attendant on Air Asia.

185. When famous artist Henri Matisse was in his 80's and partially bed

ridden, he would sketch portraits from his bed by using a 3.9 feet (1.2 meter) long stick with a pencil or piece of charcoal attached to the end in order to reach the paper or canvas.

186. A professor of medicine at Harvard Medical School is working on a new device that measures sperm concentration using your phone's camera.

187. One of the most rare blood types, type O, is shared by every single person by the Bororo people, an indigenous race in Brazil.

188. Clouds in the sky look light and fluffy, however, the water in a medium-sized cumulus cloud could weigh about 1,100,00 pounds (500,000 kilograms).

189. In Brisbane, Australia, there's a golf course with full grown bull sharks living in the water hazards.

190. On July 4, 2016, the practice of daylight saving's time was annulled by Egypt, three days before it was due to start.

191. The toughest and hardest substance in the human body is tooth enamel, not our bones as we may think. Dental enamel has to withstand heat and cold, as well as biting into hard materials. It is the most mineralized substance in our bodies and it protects the inner portions of the teeth from damage and decay.

192. In California, there is a replica of the 1948 original In-N-Out Burger at its original location on the intersection of Francis Guido and Garvey in Baldwin Park. It contains a cigarette machine, the original potato dicer, and a frying station.

193. A moonbow or lunar rainbow is a type of rainbow that can be seen at night and happens very rarely. In order for this to happen, a full moon is needed, it must be raining opposite to the moon, the sky must be dark, and the moon must be less than forty two degrees high.

194. A French woman named Nadine Vaujour was so determined to get her husband out of jail that she learned how to fly a helicopter to get him out. She succeeded in picking him up off the roof, however, was arrested shortly after.

195. There is a pee repellent paint used to protect public walls from bodily fluids, as it causes urine to splash back at the offender. In fact, San Francisco is using this paint inspired by Hamburg, Germany, who painted all their city walls with this repellent and saw public urination drop significantly.

196. Limbal dermoids are a type of tumor that can grow on the eyeball. They are made of connective tissue, skin, fat, hair, teeth, cartilage, and even bone.

197. Lyme disease got its name from Lyme, Connecticut, as it was the place where researchers found a large number of children suffering from juvenile rheumatoid arthritis, back in 1975.

198. People who wake up late at night are more likely to display antisocial personality traits, such as machiavellianism and narcissism, as well as to have more psychopathic tendencies. This was evidenced during a study done by Doctor Peter Jonassen from the University of Western Sydney in 2013.

199. The sub-Alpine reaches of Mount Kaputar, Australia, is home of the giant pink slug. They can reach up to eight inches (twenty centimeters) long and on a good day, you can actually see hundreds of them.

200. The University College of London found that teenagers are less likely to be empathetic than adults due to the continual development of their brains. Their neural area that is associated with empathy and guilt when they're making decisions is not being used to full capacity.

201. Horror movie soundtracks sometimes involve infrasound, which is sound below the range of human hearing; although we can't hear it, it's possible to feel it. Infrasound has been proven to induce anxiety, heart palpitations, and even shivering.

202. The longest running Broadway of all show performances is "The Phantom of the Opera." As of 2015, the show has had over 11,000 performances since its conception in 1988.

203. On May 20, 2016, a man named Aaron Chervenak drove all the way from Los Angeles to a little chapel in Las Vegas to get married to his smartphone.

204. Female giraffes urinate in males' mouths before mating. From the taste of her urine, the male can conclude if she is in heat or not.

205. Although Michael Jordan has never played for the Miami Heat, number twenty three was retired by the team.

206. In 2010, a computer programmer bought two large pizzas and paid ten thousand Bitcoins. If he'd kept those a little longer, they'd be worth one hundred million dollars today.

207. None of the members of The Beatles could actually read music. Music for them was a discovery process and did not involve any books.

208. In Japan, death row prisoners aren't told the date of their execution, so every single day they wake up wondering if today may be their last.

209. In the Netherlands, there is McDonald's that has a place mat called a McTrax, where you can make music while you eat. The way it works is by placing your phone on the mat, getting an app, and then composing your music including your voice.

210. Platypuses don't have stomachs. In fact, they're not the only animals without one. Others include the echidna and the carp.

211. In front of the National Gallery of Canada, in Ottawa, there is a bronze statue of a spider designed by artist Louise Bourgeois. It's called "Maman" and it cost a whopping $3.2 million. The statue measures thirty feet (nine meters) high, weighs over 13,000 pounds (5,900 kilograms), and has twenty-six white marble eggs in a sack on its underbelly.

212. Cigarettes used to be sold in vending machines that only accepted quarters and cost twenty three cents. Instead of cigarette companies increasing the price, they included two pennies inside of each box.

213. In 1923, an American jockey named Frank Hayes suffered a fatal heart attack and died mid-race. His body remained on the horse until crossing the finish line in first place. It was actually the first race he won.

214. According to the Guinness World Records, 1,416 Toyota cars were parked together at Kuznetsova airport, in Russia, on June 7, 2014, to create a giant Toyota logo, breaking the previous world record held by

Subaru. The exhibition was intended to introduce a new Toyota dealership in the area.

215. The first successful penile transplant was performed on May 15, 2016, in the United States. The recipient was sixty four year old Thomas Manning, from Massachusetts. The surgery lasted around fifteen hours and they used the penis from a deceased donor.

216. According to the results from an online survey, 11% of Americans think that HTML is a type of STD.

217. Gangaram Mahes was a homeless man in New York throughout the 1990's who would get sent to prison on purpose so he could receive three meals and a clean bed.

218. In 2015, a Russian suicide bomber had the intention of killing hundreds in Moscow on New Year's Eve. The plan failed as she received a text message from the wireless carrier wishing her a Happy New Year, which triggered the belt bomb and killed her alone.

219. There is a special watch that keeps time with Martian solar days designed by watchmaker Garo Ansertian and used by NASA. The Martian day is a bit longer than Earth's, but this minimal variance can amount to physical and mental fatigue. Everyday team members are reporting to work thirty-nine minutes later than the previous day, so the watch is actually 24.65 hours.

220. In Peru, the inhabitants of the Chumbivilcas Province celebrate a tradition on Christmas, where all the men settle grudges with each other by calling them out and having a fist fight. Afterwards they all go have drinks together to numb the pain and start the new year together.

221. As of February 2020, over two billion iPhones were sold by Apple.

222. On September 21, 1990, the Shiawassee Police Department in Michigan staged a fake wedding where the bride and groom were undercover cops who invited local drug dealers to their big day. At the reception, they busted them all at once.

223. The smallest species of armadillo is the pink fairy armadillo. It is

only four inches (ten centimeters) long, weighs about a hundred grams, and is pink in color.

224. South Korea has a population of almost fifty million people. About 20% of them have the family name of Kim; that's over ten million people.

225. A bloodhound who hunts by scent is only able to follow the scent of blood that is several days old.

226. Kakslauttanen Arctic Resort is a hotel in Finland that offers accommodation in glass igloos.

227. After saving someone for drowning, lifeguard Thomas Lopez from South Florida was actually fired. The reason why was because the man he saved wasn't technically in his assigned lifeguard area.

228. When taken by a predator, most grasshoppers will vomit a repugnant, bitter acidic bile as a last alternative defense mechanism.

229. Giraffe Manor is not only a giraffe sanctuary in Kenya, but it's also a hotel where guests can hang out with giraffes and feed them from their windows.

230. On the night of January 27, 1993, Andre the Giant died in a hotel room in Paris. Coincidentally, he was in Paris to attend his father's funeral.

231. In the movie Alfred Hitchcock's "Psycho," the blood in the famous shower scene was actually Hersey's chocolate syrup. At the time, this was the usual substance for blood in black and white films.

232. In Chile, some parts of the Atacama Desert have not seen a drop of water since record keeping began.

233. In Japan, if you are in someone's home, you need to wear slippers when walking around. Not only that, but there is one pair to be used around the house and another pair just for the bathroom.

234. The state slogan for New Hampshire is "Live Free or Die" and is written on all car license plates. Ironically these licenses are made by the prisoners of the state.

235. There are three different types of tears: basal tears keep your eyes lubricated; irritant or reflex tears are produced when you get something in your eye; and emotional tears, produced during moments of intense feeling.

236. There is an annual sidewalk egg frying contest held in Oatman, Arizona, on the 4th of July. Contenders have to fry two eggs using only solar power in a period of fifteen minutes. Mirrors, magnifying glasses, and aluminum are allowed for use to help speed up the process.

237. Major league baseballs are actually stitched by hand. In total, 108 stitches cover a single ball.

238. In December of 2000, the Netherlands became the first country to legalize same sex marriage. Today over twenty three major countries have legalized it, including Canada, England, and the United States.

239. In 2013, a man in Michigan whose house was set to be demolished, switched his house numbers with his neighbor. The company in charge of the operation ended up demolishing the wrong house.

240. During the 1997 Asian financial crisis, Koreans donated billions of dollars' worth of gold jewelry to help pay down the country's international monetary fund debt, which enabled them to pay off the debt ahead of schedule. Citizens were asked to donate their gold jewelry by the government, and many did so by donating heirlooms, wedding rings, trophies, and small gold figurines. Within a few months, about 227 tons of gold was collected.

241. Hiroo Onoda, an imperial Japanese army officer, remained at his jungle post on the island of the Philippines for twenty nine years as he refused to believe that World War II was over. He finally returned to Japan in 1974 and was welcomed as a hero.

242. Robert F. Kennedy (a former attorney general) actually failed third grade and attended almost a dozen schools. He was smaller than his siblings and was often considered the runt of the family.

243. The term "Captcha" means Completely Automated Public Turing Test to Tell Computers and Humans Apart.

244. In 2013, PayPal put over $92 quadrillion into executive Chris Reynolds' account by mistake. They soon admitted their error and offered to donate money to a cause of Reynolds' choice.

245. Koalas drink water very rarely. In general, the water they drink comes from gum leaves or from dew or rainwater on the surface of the leaves. Over 90% of their hydration is received from the eucalyptus leaves that they eat. They only drink when ill or at times when there isn't enough moisture on the leaves, like during very dry weather.

246. In 1984, Jack Lalanne, known also as the "Godfather of Fitness," towed seventy rowboats with passengers in them from Queensway Bridge to the ship Queen Mary while shackled, handcuffed, and fighting winds and currents. He achieved this on his seventieth birthday.

247. During World War I, a flock of forty-eight sheep were kept by Woodrow Wilson on the White House lawn to save money on groundskeepers. The sheep also collected over fifty thousand dollars for the Red Cross through the auction of their wool.

248. The idea for the movie "The Human Centipede" came from a joke between the director and writer on what should happen to child molesters.

249. Nat-2 is a German sneaker company that has created the first vegan wooden sneaker. They are made of up to 90% real sustainable wood, which is applied to an organic cotton and vector engraved in a way that the material bends and becomes soft and flexible, like fine leather.

250. In Vietnam, eating still-beating hearts of live cobras is considered a delicacy.

251. In March of 2017, a hamburger sold at a charity auction in Dubai for $10,000. It contained seven beef patties, one for each of the emirates in The United Arab Emirates, aged cheddar cheese, and veal bacon strips in a saffron brioche bun.

252. There has only been a total of 260 years of peace since the beginning of recorded history.

253. In order to scare off birds, the Gloucestershire Airport in England used to blast Tina Turner music. It was proved to work even better than blasting bird distress calls.

254. In the village of Ziembark, Poland, there is a house that is completely upside down. It was designed as an artwork to represent the end of the communist era in Poland, by Polish businessman and philanthropist Daniel Sirpaski. The house was finished in 2007 and took almost five times longer than a conventional house to construct.

255. The first woman to vie for the presidency was Victory Woodhull, in 1872, running as an equal rights party nominee against Ulysses S. Grant. This happened fifty years before the 19th amendment that gave women the right to vote.

256. In the movie "Saving Private Ryan," some combat scenes looked so realistic that veterans actually had to leave the movie theaters during the opening scene; they stated that it was the most realistic depiction of combat that they had ever seen.

257. A nurdle is the name given to that blob of toothpaste in the shape of a wave on your toothpaste box.

258. A man named Daryl Davis befriended some members of the KKK in the 1980's which caused them to leave the group as they slowly learned all the misconceptions of the black community.

259. In 2003, when a Coca-Cola employee was caught drinking Pepsi on the job, he was immediately fired.

260. In 2016, for the first time in 108 years, the Chicago Cubs won the World Series.

261. There is a three volume book called the "Principia Mathematica" which details the foundations of mathematics. In the book there is proof that one plus one equals two, that is over a hundred and fifty pages long.

262. According to recent scientific findings, the five tastes or senses that your tongue can recognize are sweet, sour, salty, bitter, and umami. Parmesan cheese is an example of umami.

263. The stripes on tigers are on their skin and not just their fur.

264. On February 2, 2017, a world record for visiting every country in the world in the fastest time was set by twenty seven year old Cassie De Pecol from Connecticut. She left on July 24, 2015, and visited all 196 countries in just eighteen and a half months.

265. When Paris' sewers get clogged, officials often use large wood and iron rolling balls to clean them out, the same technique used over a hundred years ago.

266. According to the American College of Allergy, Asthma, and Immunology, if you get bitten by a lone star tick, you are vulnerable to develop an allergy to red meat, including beef and pork. The allergy symptoms may include a stuffy and running nose, nausea, and skin rash after eating meat.

267. Leonidas is depicted as a young man of about thirty in the Battle of Thermopylae in the movie 300, however, in reality he was closer to sixty.

268. In rich countries, obesity is more common among the less educated. In poor countries on the contrary, obesity is common among the highly educated.

269. In Vicenza, Italy, a grandmother accidentally sent five people to hospital, two adults and three children. She made them cocoa without knowing that the packets had expired back in 1990.

270. The record for a human intentionally staying awake without the use of any stimulants is held by sixteen year old high school student Randy Gardner. He stayed awake for eleven days and twenty four minutes, in 1965. That's 265 hours straight.

271. A study done by psychologist Adrian Furnham found that perfectionism can lead to depression. Often, perfectionists have unrealistic views of failure and are overly critical of themselves, leading to them having a negative impact on their day to day lives.

272. In 2016, Budweiser changed its name to America. Labels on all bottles and cans were changed, with images and phrases related to the United States. The controversial campaign was called "America in Your Hands" and it ran from May 23 to November, 2016.

273. Kim Kardashian used to be Paris Hilton's personal assistant back in the mid-2000's.

274. In the 1930's, McDonald's started off selling hotdogs from a cart. Today, the fast food giant sells seventy five hamburgers every second of every day.

275. There is a species of recently discovered nocturnal lizards that are found only on Madagascar. The Geckolepis megalepis is a kind of fish-scaled gecko and has an amazing defense mechanism. When grabbed by a predator, it can shed patches of skin and scales from most of its body, causing the scales to get stuck in the attacker's mouths.

276. In 2016, a year of unlimited data was given by T-Mobile to all its customers to play Pokémon GO. Additionally, they offered 50% off mobile accessories such as portable power packs and other items because so many people's phones were dying.

277. Female mosquitoes are the only ones to bite humans and animals. Male mosquitoes on the contrary only feed themselves on flower nectar.

278. Lemurs have extremely bad vision. In fact, they are only able to see in black and white.

279. To combat speeding drivers, inhabitants of a village named Hope-man, in Scotland, have been posing as police officers using speed guns by arming themselves with hair dryers and reflective vests.

280. The largest known diamond in the universe discovered by astronomers is a star named Lucy, shaped by ten trillion billion karats. This white dwarf has a carbon interior that crystallized as it cooled, forming a giant diamond in the sky. The star was named by scientists after The Beatles' song "Lucy in the Sky with Diamonds."

281. The LG in "LG Corporation" stands for Lucky Goldstar, which is its former name and it is also the acronym of the company's tagline: "Life's Good."

282. The most expensive bottle of vodka in the world costs almost four million dollars. It's filtered through sand and created from crushed up gems and diamonds.

283. Catfish have about 100,000 taste buds spread all over their bodies, most of them located on their whiskers.

284. One of the oldest cities in the world is Jerusalem which has been attacked over fifty times, destroyed twice, and captured and then recaptured over forty times.

285. Berserk male syndrome is a condition that male llamas and alpacas can suffer from. Owners suddenly find their animals wildly charging at them from behind or rearing up at them, screaming, spitting, and biting. It's caused by human over handling and when the alpaca or llama begins to look at their human as a rival.

286. There are some species of turtles where the temperature determines whether the egg will develop into a male or female. In lower temperatures, the egg will develop into a male turtle, while in higher temperatures, the egg will develop into a female.

287. There is a type of HIV test that uses a USB stick developed by scientists at Imperial College London and US firm DNA Electronics. Using a drop of blood to detect HIV, it then creates an electrical signal that can be read by a computer, laptop, or handheld device.

288. According to a survey conducted in the US, 51% of people consider that sharing a Netflix password with a significant other means the relationship is serious.

289. When cats rub their face on something, they leave their own scent behind as they have glands located around their mouths, chins, inside of their face, neck, and ears. This is called bunting.

290. The urine of bear cats actually smells like buttered popcorn. In fact, their urine has the same compound that is found in buttered popcorn.

291. Studies have actually proven that opposites do attract. A couple having too much in common is more likely not to last as long together. On the contrary, having different opinions while still respecting your partners is healthier in relationships.

292. In Alaska, attorney and MIT alum Phillip Weidner has built what

is called the Goose Creek Tower and what the locals call the Dr. Seuss house. It began as a 39.3 by 39.3 feet (twelve-by-twelve meter) log cabin, but he kept joining one log cabin after the other on top of each other. The log cabins progressively get smaller and the tower has reached almost eighty-two feet (fifty-five meters) tall. The only reason that he stopped was because federal airspace starts at 200 feet (sixty-one meters).

293. During the 2007 writer's strike, the Late Show staff was actually paid out by David Letterman's own pocket.

294. There is a doll created for Nivea that is made of UV-sensitive material. The doll turns into a painful-looking bright red if left out in the sun, so applying sunscreen to it turns it white again. It was made with the purpose of teaching children the importance of wearing sunscreen.

295. Most gladiators were vegetarians. Their diets used to consist mainly of barley and vegetables.

296. R.L. Stine, the legendary horror writer, started his career by writing comics for Bazooka Joe Bubble Gum; his pen name was Jovial Bob Stein.

297. In 1824, while being only fifteen years old, Louis Braille developed the Braille system. He actually became blind at the age of three and was inspired to find a way for the blind to read and write.

298. Based on statistics, more people have died from selfies than shark attacks.

299. Based on reports issued by the World Health Organization, about 265,000 people die every year from burns that occur mostly at home or the workplace.

300. When feeling threatened, the mimosa pudica plant native to Central and South America, also known as touch-me-not plant, plays dead. If it's touched by a predator, its stems release a chemical that causes leaves to shrivel up. Once the danger is gone, it comes back to life.

301. In Lancaster, California, there is a musical road that was created as a TV ad for Honda. The road is cut into groves that when traveling about fifty miles (eighty kilometers) per hour, it will play William Tell's Overture.

302. In 1972, Shirley Chisholm became the first black woman to run for the presidency in the US. Although she never expected to win, she ran only to prove that Americans could vote for a black woman.

303. Archeologists found what they think are the oldest pieces of chewing gum, at Orust Island in Sweden, in 1993. They dated back more than 9,000 years, and they were three bits of chewed birch resin.

304. Drug smugglers dropped approximately eighty eight pounds (forty kilograms) of cocaine into the Chattahoochee National Forest in Georgia, in 1985. A black bear stumbled upon the drugs, ate all of them, and died a while later because of a serious overdose. The bear got the nickname Pablo Escobar.

305. Even though we associate Cleopatra with the Egyptian Great Pyramid, the fact is that she lived during times that were closer to the invention of smartphones than the construction of those gigantic ancient wonders of the world. Wooly mammoths were still walking around at the time when the Great Pyramid was finished.

306. Although gothic architecture is often linked with vampires, one of its core design principles is to let in as much natural light as possible.

307. Roger Lausier almost drowned in 1965, but was saved by a woman named Alice Blaise. Nine years afterwards, Lausier was on a raft on the same beach, when he pulled a drowning man out of the water, and he later realized that he had saved Alice's husband.

308. Compared to coffee, apples are more effective in waking you up during the morning. The fruit gives you glucose, which energizes the body, and provides fuel to the brain.

309. If your eyes were as good as the Hubble Space Telescopes' Wide Field and Planetary Camera, you'd be able to read standard fine print newspaper pages from more than one mile (1.6 kilometers) away.

310. The standard Google logo was replaced by a Google doodle, which was some kind of out-of-office message, for the first time on August 30, 1998. It was a stick figure of a Burning Man that was meant to let users know that Google founders Sergey and Larry weren't available to fix any issues or bugs, because they had gone to Nevada for the Burning Man Festival.

311. There are ambulances that are called to come and help when trees are infected with fungi, insects or pests in India. The ambulance is stocked with fungicides, pesticides and insecticides.

312. Will Ferrell refused to take twenty nine million dollars to make a sequel for Elf. He thought that if the movie wasn't great, he couldn't deal with being criticized by people who'd think he'd just made the movie for the cash.

313. Rock band Blink 182 was originally called "Duct Tape."

314. A plant that produces two unique edible crops have been created by a UK-based horticulture firm called Thompson & Morgan. It's called the "TomTato," and one plant can produce 4.4 pounds (two kilograms) of potatoes and 500 tomato fruits in a single planting season.

315. When male fireflies are fully grown, they never eat their food because they have a strong drive to mate, and they have a short life span to accomplish that. Certain female fireflies can copy the blinking rates of other species of firefly, attracting the males that want to mate, only to end up eating them instead.

316. Disneyland sells almost three million churros at their parks every year.

317. In the eight year span of Kareen Abdul Jabbar's high school and college basketball career, he managed to win 212 matches, and only lost eight. He also won the championship every single year where he was eligible.

318. Renowned musician Yo-Yo Ma accidentally left his cello, which was 266 years old and worth $2.5 million, in a taxi trunk in 1999. The police were able to find it at a garage in Queens, right on time for a concert scheduled for that night.

319. The KLF, a British electronic band, declared that they were quitting the music business on February 12, 1992, at the Brit Awards. At the end of their set, Bill Drummond shot a machine gun with blanks over the heads of the bewildered audience. After the ceremony, he and fellow bandmates left a dead sheep at the doorway, with a note that said, "I died for you, bon appetit."

320. The average person produces two swimming pools worth of saliva in their mouth in a lifetime.

321. Infertile mice were able to give birth after they were implanted with ovaries that were artificially created with three-dimensional printers, on May 17, 2017. Ultimately, the hope is that the ovarian bioprosthesis procedure could work on humans.

322. Within the time that they were starring as brother and sister on the Showtime program Dexter, Jennifer Carpenter and Michael C. Hall started going out, got engaged, became married, and got divorced.

323. They used to charge three half-pence to admit visitors into the London Zoo back in the eighteenth century. However, those who didn't have the money could be let in if they brought a dog or a cat as food for the lions.

324. In the UK, you can get your ashes baked into a vinyl record by a company called "And Vinyly" after you are cremated. The record can even contain songs you like, your own voice, or an audio version of your will.

325. Ireland has some really weird laws that have been in place for centuries. One states that if a leprechaun shows up at your doorstep, you have to share your dinner with him.

326. The White House had its first electric lighting installed in 1891. Then President Benjamin Harrison was so scared of getting electrocuted, that he completely refused to touch any of the light switches to turn them on or off.

327. The flame and fury PF24-007 peach is the biggest kind of peach in the world. They were originally grown in Colome, Michigan, at Paul

Friday Farms. When mature, they measure three inches (7.6 centimeters) in diameter.

328. Nottingham Trent University's Dr. Martin Bencsik discovered that when honeybees bump into each other, they emit vibrations which sound remarkably like whoops. He and his peers believed that the sound indicates that the bees are startled.

329. Richard Montanez was a janitor working at a factory floor, when the idea for Frito-Lay's Flamin Hot Cheetos came to him. He invented the product, and today, he works at Pepsi-Co as an executive vice president.

330. When a human adult is bitten by a Russell's pit viper, he can go through what seems like reverse puberty. The snake is native to Southeast Asia, and its venom can destroy someone's pituitary gland, to the extent that it stops secreting hormones. As a result, the person may lose their fertility, sex drive, and body hair. That's if the snake bite doesn't actually kill the person.

331. The Republic of Nauru has the biggest percentage of obese citizens as per the World Health Organization. Around 94.5% of their entire population is overweight according to a 2007 report. The United States is ninth in terms of obesity, with 74.1% of people being overweight.

332. The Ewoks' language was created by Ben Burtt, a sound designer for the Star Wars franchise. It's mostly a bunch of Tibetan phrases and a little Nepalese.

333. Natalia Karp was born in Poland, and was sent to a concentration camp in 1943 after losing her husband in a bombing raid. At the camp, she saved hers and her sister's lives, by skillfully playing Nocturne in C Sharp Minor by Chopin on piano, and impressing the camp's commandant who chose to spare the two.

334. After Leland Stanford and his wife lost their fifteen year old son unexpectedly, they decided that the only thing they could do for him was to memorialize him. They therefore founded Stanford University, a place where California's children could also be their children.

335. "Presidentress" was the official word used to refer to the president's wife, until 1849 in Dolly Madison's eulogy when Zachary Taylor referred to her as "our first lady."

336. The total weight of all the bones in a pigeon is lower than the weight of its feathers.

337. In most cultures, sticking out one's tongue is considered a sign of distaste. However, in Tibet, it has the opposite meaning, because sticking your tongue at someone is considered good manners.

338. A pilot named Linda Ducharme held a vow renewal ceremony in 2013 with Bruce, a Ferris wheel that she had already married. She fed a piece of pizza to the Ferris wheel during the ceremony, which was officiated by a Catholic priest who declared "I tie you flesh and steel."

339. There was a place in Auschwitz called Canada, and it's where valuable items taken from prisoners were stored. It got the name because, in that era, the country of Canada was said to have many untold riches.

340. The word fruit refers to the component of a plant which comes from a flower, and the part that contains seeds. The remaining parts, including leaves, stems, and flower buds, are considered vegetables. Therefore, beans, tomatoes, cucumbers, and avocados are all fruits.

341. A thirty seven year old Scottish man from Glasgow set the world record for suffering the longest hangover. He consumed more than sixty pints (thirty five liters) of beer in a span of four days, and he ended up having serious hydration symptoms for the next four weeks. He had to see a specialist who put him on blood thinning treatments for six whole months, and after that, his headaches and blurred visions eventually subsided.

342. Campbell soup offers a watercress and duck gizzard flavored product in Hong Kong, China, and a cream of Chile poblano flavored product in Mexico.

343. Limes sink in most cases when placed in a pool of water, but lemons float. Orange fruits will float when they are whole, but they'll sink when they are in slices.

344. A small town in Iowa called Riverside declared in 1985, that it was the future birthplace of original Star Trek series character James Tiberius Kirk, who was the captain of USS Enterprise.

345. When a woman reaches her early thirties, her fertility starts to decline, and it speeds up when she gets to thirty five. She only has a 5% chance of getting pregnant during any particular month from the age of forty. This happens because women are born with all the eggs they are ever going to have throughout their lives, so as they age, the eggs age too, and they reduce both in number and quality.

346. Portobello, cremini, and the button mushrooms are actually the exact same type of mushroom, and are just at different states of maturity.

347. The longest civil war in world history is still going on. It's called the Karen Conflict, and it started in Karen State, Burma, in 1949, now known as Karen State, Myanmar. Currently, Karen State Nationalists are engaged in a fight with Myanmar Armed Forces, and they want independence.

348. On average, people spend over three months of their lives on toilets with men spending four minutes longer than women on toilets every day.

349. The word "Beastie" in the band name The Beastie Boys is short for "Boys Entertaining Anarchistic States towards Inner Excellence."

350. People who hold the belief that human life can be sustained minus water and food but merely by prana, are known as breatharians. Prana is what's known as life force, and it's the light and air around a person. Many breatharians claim that they have lived for extended periods of time without water and food, but unfortunately, some people have died trying to replicate their example.

351. Hayley Atwell, who portrays Marvel character Peggy Carter in the Captain America movies, took a driver's license photo in April, 2015, while wearing her full movie makeup.

352. When you sprinkle your pineapple with salt, it becomes sweeter. It's because table salt is mainly sodium chlorine, and the sodium is effective

in lowering bitterness levels in foods, so it makes the pineapple less bitter.

353. In New York State, you legally have to let a buyer know if a house is considered haunted before you sell it to them.

354. European settlers gave Argentina its name because they suspected that there were hidden riches within the mountains. The word Argentina loosely translates to "silvery" in Italian. There was a legend about a hidden mountain of silver in that land at the time.

355. Your heart will beat roughly three billion times if you are fortunate enough to live the average length of a human life.

356. "The Modern Toilet" is a restaurant in Taipei, Taiwan, that has a gross theme, which it pushes to the extreme. Their food is served in bowls in the shape of toilets, and their drinks are distributed in urine sample bottles. Their menu offers food like stuffed brown sugar poop pancakes, poop meatballs, and patrons eat while seated on toilets.

357. Eugene Shoemaker, a planetary scientist who died in 1997, is the only human that's buried on the moon. NASA's Lunar Prospector went to the moon's South Pole on a mission to find water on January 6, 1998, and it carried an urn with Shoemaker's ashes. On July 1, 1999, the same spacecraft was deliberately crashed into the surface of the moon, thus making Shoemaker the first person to be buried off-world.

358. The vast majority of the Muppets of the Muppet Show or Sesame Street are left handed. This is a result of the fact that most puppeteers are right-handed. They therefore tend to use their right hand to control the puppets' mouths, and the left hand to control the puppets' left limb or hand rod.

359. If you come across Bigfoot when you are down in Texas, you have a legal right to shoot him dead, according to state laws. On the other side, there are some places such as Skamania County in Washington where it's legally forbidden to kill a Sasquatch.

360. Oxbotica Company developed self-driving cars by teaching them to navigate using a series of software programs, including Grand Theft Auto Five. The company used GTA to simulate driving conditions

because, as it claims, "there isn't enough time in a day to clock the real world miles that they needed."

361. In 1998, Florida passed a law that mandated that all state-funded preschools and daycare facilities should play classical music for the kids. They originally thought that the Mozart effect would contribute to the development of the children's minds, but although that effect was disapproved, the law still remains in place to date.

362. The Maldives would be the first country to vanish if oceans rise because of global warming. It's an island country that's also the flattest on Earth, and none of its land is more than nine feet (three meters) above sea level.

363. The world became increasingly more generous between 2001 and 2011, as per the 2012 Giving USA Report. Charitable giving around the globe grew by 240% within that decade.

364. The first street in the world to be lit by gas lights was Pall Mall, in 1807, in London. The street still exists today, but modern lamp posts are used in place of gas lights.

365. "Virgule" is the technical name for the forward slash.

366. During the anti-Sikh riots that occurred between October 31 and November 3, 1984, more than 2,800 Sikhs were killed. Some reports indicate that the numbers were much higher, closer to 8,000 in total, and roughly 3,000 within Delhi alone.

367. Nerf, the toy company, first started its slogan as "Nerf, throw it indoors, you can't damage lamps, or break windows, you can't hurt babies, or old people."

368. Vulcan Point Island is located in the Philippines, within a lake, that's within an active volcano, that's within a bigger lake, that's within a much bigger island.

369. An Aquatic Biologist named Tim Wong, of the San Francisco California Academy of Sciences, personally repopulated and saved the California Pipeline Swallowtail butterfly species by breeding them in a greenhouse behind his house.

370. The metal lubricant WD-40 has many other uses. For instance, it can kill insects and cockroaches, and you can spray it over your doors, windows, and screens to keep insects out.

371. One of the founders of the Kellogg's Company which makes several popular cereals, John H Kellogg, wasn't properly educated as a child because his parents didn't believe their kids needed education, as they were certain that Christ would come back before they grew up. Despite that background, John went on to get a medical degree and he founded a food company whose products are eaten in millions of homes.

372. "The Bergie Seltzer" is the name of the fizzing sound produced by icebergs when they melt. The sound is produced when air bubbles that have been trapped under pressure in the ice for centuries finally pop.

373. Charles Joughin, the head baker aboard RMS Titanic, managed to stay cool when the ship struck an iceberg on April 14, 1912. He asked his bakers to distribute bread to passengers on lifeboats as they awaited rescue, and he offered his seat to another person. After a drink, he started throwing chairs into the water, so that those trying to stay afloat would have something to grasp onto. He did go down with the ship and he survived in the freezing-cold water long enough to be rescued.

374. Before dynamite got its name, the explosive was called "Nobel's safety powder," and was named after Alfred Nobel, who invented it.

375. Situated on an island close to Sicily in Italy, Mount Stromboli is a volcano that's called "the Lighthouse of the Mediterranean." It has been erupting constantly for more than 2,000 years.

376. A new exhibit that showcases the world's largest collection of fossilized poop was opened on August 3, 2015, at the South Florida Museum. The largest of all the fossils was excrement from a prehistoric crocodile. It is as big as a puppy. It was nicknamed precious.

377. Chimpanzees can recognize their own fashion trends, according to research done in 2014 at a sanctuary in Zambia. Some chimps started putting bits of glass in their ears in one instance, and the only apparent reason for this was that they wanted to feel like a part of the group.

378. President John F. Kennedy had such a privileged childhood and upbringing that he said that he only found out about the Great Depression by reading books about it at Harvard.

379. Zebras and donkeys can breed with each other. When they do, the resulting crossbreed is called a Zonkey.

380. Mikhail Gorbachev, former leader of the Soviet Union, appeared in a 1997 Pizza Hut advert with Anastasia, his ten year old granddaughter. The ad used footage of the two in a Pizza Hut to argue that capitalism is preferable to communism because it made luxuries such as the restaurant available to people.

381. Vinegar eel is a real thing. It's a worm that's one sixteenth of an inch (1.6 millimeters) in length that eats living yeast and bacteria cultures that are used to make vinegar. They are present in unfiltered yeast, and they are often raised as fish feed.

382. Instead of an actual belly button, model Karolina Kurkova has a smooth indentation on her navel area, a result of a surgery she had in her infancy. They often Photoshop a belly button onto her photos to hide this.

383. In a Spanish cave in 2013, scientists discovered fossilized remains of a fractured human skull. To their astonishment, the skull belonged to a murdered young adult that lived there 43,000 years before. They think it might be the first ever murder case.

384. As a result of an ad campaign that ran in 1967, residents of Piscataqua village in Ecuador voted in a foot deodorant called "Pul Vapes" during a mayoral race.

385. The country with the youngest population in the world is Niger. It has eighteen million citizens, and almost half of them are under the age of fifteen. That's because the country has an oddly high fertility rate of 6.6 children for every woman.

386. The first president of the Equatorial Guinea, Francisco Macias Nguema, changed the country's motto to "There's no other god than Macias Nguema." He did that in 1978, and was overthrown and killed the next year.

387. Of the four Metallica band members, three of them divorced their wives while they were producing the Black album. The band believes that this contributed to the moody feeling reflected in their tracks.

388. The original version of Pac-Man, the classic arcade game, was designed to never end. However, for those proficient enough to get to level 256, the game would go haywire and that made the level impossible to win.

389. There are seventeen fictional characters who have their own stars on the Hollywood Walk of Fame. They include Mickey Mouse, Shrek, Donald Duck, Bugs Bunny, Snoopy, Woody Woodpecker, and Godzilla.

390. The US Airfare was conducting military exercises near Tybee Island near the state of Georgia, on February 5, 1958, when a B47 bomber collided with an F86 fighter in midair, and a Mark 15 nuclear bomb was subsequently lost. The nuke was not active to prevent detonation, and the military did extensive searches. It was not found and it remains lost in the Atlantic Ocean to date.

391. 12% of humans dream in black and white as per the US National Library of Medicine. Those aged twenty five or less only dream in color, and those aged fifty five or higher say they only dream in color 75% of the time.

392. The Barbie Liberation Organization was a group of activists and artists who, in 1993, performed surgery on about 300 to 500 dolls, switching the voice boxes inside the G.I Joe and the Barbie figures, returning all the toys to the stores afterwards. G.I Joes were reportedly saying things like "the beach is a great place for the summer," while Barbies were saying "vengeance is mine."

393. Because he was delusional and obsessed with Jodie Foster, John Hinckley Junior tried to assassinate President Ronald Reagan in 1981. He was released from a psychiatric institution on September 10, 2016, and he now lives with his mom.

394. Located in Hausberg, Bavaria, the Fuggerei is the oldest social housing complex in the whole world, and current renters still pay what

used to be paid when the houses were constructed in the 1500's, an amount equivalent to one American Dollar.

395. Radford Army Ammunition Plant, a top secret military explosives manufacturer in Virginia, had to take some additional precautions when in July, 2016, people started sneaking onto their property while playing the phone game Pokémon Go. There was a rumor that a Charizard had been spotted on the premises, but it wasn't true.

396. There has been a real court case called Batman V Commissioner, but it wasn't the Dark Knight suing the head of the Gotham Police force. A farmer called Ray Batman was attempting to appeal a decision by the IRS to increase his tax.

397. Elvis Presley's dark-slicked hair is one of the most recognizable things about him, but he was really a natural blonde. He chose the raven-black dyed look because he thought it made him appear edgier.

398. The sixth most populous Peruvian city is Iquitos, which serves as the capital of the Lareto Region and Maynas Province. Although it has 470,000 residents, the city is only accessible by air or by river. It's the biggest city in the world that can't be reached by road.

399. Edward Hedrick, who invented Frisbee golf, wished that when he died, his ashes would be molded into a new line of Frisbees. His last wishes were honored, and a series of Frisbees containing his ashes were sold, ensuring that he would be thrown around forever.

400. Every forty six seconds in the United States, a truck, car, or other type of vehicle is stolen, according to a report by the National Highway Traffic Safety Administration. The 1994 Honda Accord was the most stolen vehicle in 2011, as per the National Insurance Crime Bureau, and it held the same position in 2008, 2009, and 2010.

401. 500 million people were infected by the global influenza pandemic that took place from 1918 to 1919. That was about a third of Earth's population at the time, and between twenty and fifty million people died as a result of the disease.

402. Because of a glitch in the Canadian iTunes Store in 2014, Taylor Swift accidentally launched a song called Track Three. Although it was

only eight seconds of static, the song immediately reached the top of the music charts.

403. According to the penal code of the US state of South Carolina, first time domestic abuse offenders can be jailed for a maximum of thirty days, while those arrested for abusing dogs can be jailed for a maximum of five years.

404. It took Lady Gaga ten minutes each to write her sounds "Just Dance," and "Born This Way." Both songs hit number one on the charts.

405. Both your mood and your manner of thinking can be influenced by the kind of music you listen to. Research indicates that various genres of music affect you differently, with some making you more patient, others making you more confident, and some that even make it possible for you to overcome emotional trauma a lot faster.

406. In 1997, a survey done in America showed that 12% of people thought that Noah, the biblical character who built an arc, was the husband of Joan of Arc. Although both figures did receive messages from God, that's as far as their similarities go, because they didn't even live in the same era in history.

407. 80% of the press coverage of Donald Trump during his first one hundred days as president were negative according to a Harvard study.

408. The Federal Government of the United States owns one marijuana farm, which is located at the University of Mississippi campus.

409. Donnie Yen, the action star, was outside a nightclub one evening when he was attacked by eight gang members who started harassing his girlfriend. He tried to stop them, and ended up sending all of them to the hospital.

410. Diane Hartley, an architectural student, pointed out a flaw in the construction of a New York City skyscraper in 1978, and effectively saved countless lives. If she hadn't discovered the flaw, the fifty nine story structure might have collapsed on everyone inside.

411. Several famous musicians could neither read nor write music when

they first became famous singers. They include Elvis Presley, Michael Jackson, Eric Clapton, Jimi Hendrix, Eddie Van Halen, and the four members of the Beatles.

412. At the Kennedy Space Center Titusville, Florida, NASA has a vehicle assembly building that is so gigantic that it has its own weather. Because of the humidity in the building, rain clouds usually form inside it.

413. Of thirty three laparoscopic surgeons that were studied, the nine that had experience playing video games made 37% less mistakes, and they finished their procedures 27% faster than the other twenty four who hardly ever played video games.

414. UCLA scientists used MRI scanners to determine that when people felt heartbroken e.g. at the end of a relationship, the parts of their brains that lit up were the same ones that did when they felt physical pain.

415. When ants die, they lay for two whole days on that spot, before the other ants in the colony carry them and put them on a heap of other dead ants.

416. Instead of paying his secretaries, Salvador Dali chose to offer them commission. As a result, they ended up making seven figures many years later.

417. Scholars believe that the symbol "@" dates back hundreds of years ago, and was invented by monks.

418. Graphologist Cathy McKnight claims that experts could discover more than 5,000 personality traits of an individual, just by studying his or her handwriting. She says that individuals who write in large letters are typically outgoing and desire to be noticed, while those who prefer small letters tend to be more introverted, but have a stronger ability to focus or concentrate.

419. As German and Russian soldiers were fighting during the First World War in the winter of 1916 to 1917, they were attacked by a massive pack of starving wolves. Things got so bad that the two enemy

sides agreed to work together temporarily, just to survive the vicious animals.

420. The practice of brides standing on the left side of the altar originates back to the days of "marriage by capture." Back then, the groom had to keep his right hand free so he could use it to fight or fend off competitors making a last attempt to swipe away his bride.

421. The Mahabharata is the longest poem ever written, and it's a text that's meant to explain Hinduism principles. It has 74,000 verses, totaling 1.8 million words and would take you two whole weeks to finish it if you recited it non-stop.

422. Alcatraz was a maximum high security federal prison that was home to the most notorious criminals, but it was also known for the great food that it served its inmates. Murderers serving more than one life sentence often ate baked meat croquettes, beef steaks, and cupcakes with icing. They were permitted to eat as much food as they wanted, provided they didn't leave any waste behind.

423. Vampire bat saliva contains draculin, a glycoprotein that's named after count Dracula, and serves as an anticoagulant that enables the bats to feed on blood. It's applied through the bat's bite, and it stops blood from clotting, so the bats are able to drink it a lot faster.

424. Paranormal Activity, the horror movie, made $194 million, although it was filmed with a budget of just $15,000.

425. MIT mails out acceptance notices each year on March 14, which is called "Pi Day," at 6.28pm, which is known as "Tau Time."

426. Male hippos spin their tails around in order to fling their feces. They do this to attract female hippos, and also to mark their territory.

427. The company that made the game "Cards against Humanity" wanted to protect people from the madness of Black Friday shopping in 2014, so they chose to avoid putting out a new product, and instead, they sold and sent out 30,000 boxes containing bull excrement.

428. Hurricane Harvey caused so much rainfall in the American South on August 28, 2017, it forced the National Weather Service to add two

new colors: light purple and dark purple, to their graphical reports because the flood water had more than doubled the fifteen inch maximum, represented by a dark red indicator.

429. In a link posted to their Facebook page as an April Fool's Day prank in 2014, NPR (National Public Radio) accused Americans of not reading things anymore. Outraged people quickly posted slews of comments, but the few who actually clicked the link and read the content, found a congratulatory message. NPR proved that many people commented on posts without actually reading them, even when the topic was about reading.

430. Danny DeVito voiced the main character in "The Lorax," which was released in 2012. The actor also voiced the same character in the Italian, Spanish, German, and Russian dubbed version of the animated film.

431. There are twenty two emojis carved into the concrete façade of a building in Amersfoort in the Netherlands. The design was done by the Attika Architekten Dutch architectural company.

432. Steve Jobs wanted actor Jeff Goldblum to voice Siri, but when Goldblum received the request from Jobs on the phone, he thought it was someone else, and he turned down the offer.

433. Hollywood star Morgan Freeman was in a car accident in 2008, where he broke his elbow, arm, and shoulder. He was in surgery for four hours, but afterwards, his left fingers remained paralyzed. He has to keep wearing a compression glove so that blood keeps flowing in his hand.

434. California generated so much solar power in 2016, that they literally paid Arizona to take the surplus.

435. Lots of people relocate to Florida after retirement, and the trend is so popular that by 2030, an estimated one out of four Florida residents will be over sixty five years old.

436. In 2000, during the prime of Blockbuster Video stores, the company made about $800 million from collecting late fees, which accounted for 16% of their revenue.

437. As a general rule, there must be some form of food within 150 feet (forty five meters) of all parts of Google offices.

438. If you are a man in America, you are five times more likely to be killed by lightning than your female counterparts, according to America's National Health Protection Agency. Data from 1968 to 2010 showed that 85% of the 3,389 people killed by lightning strikes were male.

439. A two-lane road could be constructed between the cities of New York and San Francisco, just by using the same amount of cement that went into constructing the Hoover Dam.

440. Author Michael Crichton suspected that his Harvard English professor was giving him unfair grades, so to prove his suspicions, he submitted a George Orwell essay as his own. The professor gave the essay a B minus.

441. "Vortex I" was an event hosted from August 27 to September 3, 1970, in Clackamas County, Oregon, and was attended by tens of thousands of people. It was a free biodegradable festival of life, and to date, is still the only large scale rock event in America that was facilitated by a republican governor. However, it turned out that the entire event was an elaborate plan to keep the youth away from a Portland convention that then president Richard Nixon attended, and the plan actually worked.

442. In five coordinated attacks in 1985, the Aum Shinrikyo cult, in Japan, released sarin gas on three metro lines in Tokyo during rush hour. Twelve people died as a result, and fifty others were seriously injured with some dying later. More than 200 cult members were arrested and thirteen senior leaders were executed after receiving death sentences.

443. In Basel, Switzerland, in 1474, a rooster laid an egg, and as a result the whole community panicked because they believed it was Satan's work. The rooster was put on trial, found guilty and burned alive, but they later discovered that it was just a hen that looked remarkably like a rooster.

444. On June 26, 1974, a black and white barcode was scanned for the

first time ever, on a product in a supermarket in Troy, Ohio. The scanned product was a pack of Juicy Fruit Gum from the company Wrigley's.

445. "Gnus" are also called wildebeests. They start learning to walk just minutes after birth, and can follow their mothers around and herd in a matter of days.

446. To attract female peacocks, the male ones make fake mating sounds. This makes sexually active females assume that the male is mating, although they aren't. It works by making the females believe that the male one is more genetically fit than his rivals.

447. In the Island of Tanna, there is a remote village named Yaohnanen where they worship Prince Phillip as a god, and they are currently waiting for him to go there and live among them. A prophet from the island claimed that he had a vision of a great event that would happen in the future and capture the attention of the world.

448. William Shatner, the iconic Canadian actor, revealed that he and his fellow Star Trek actor DeForest Kelly, avoided talking to each other for two years, after he laughed upon hearing Kelly's sad story about Emily, his Chihuahua, who ran into a sprinkler head on and was killed instantly.

449. American businessman Russ George partnered with Haida Salmon Restoration Company in October, 2012, to pour a hundred tons of iron sulphate off the British Columbia, Canada coast, into the Pacific Ocean. This was done to boost the growth of planktons which are known to absorb carbon dioxide from the air.

450. Lake Superior, which is located on American's northern border with Canada, is the third largest freshwater lake in the world. It contains enough water to cover both North America and South America to a depth of about one foot (thirty centimeters).

451. The pistol shrimp is able to stun its prey by using its claws. They have a large claw and when they snap it shut, it creates an intense burst of sound that stuns its prey. In addition, they have a punch that is even

faster than a 0.22 caliber bullet, which literally smashes their prey into pieces.

452. The Puck Fair is one of the oldest annual festivals in Ireland, and it happens between August 10 and 12, in Killorgrin Town. During the event, they always capture a wild goat from the mountain and carry it down. It's then crowned King Puck, and it's put on a pedestal in a small cage for the duration of the festival, before they let it go free.

453. The Orkney Viking ruler, Yarl Siggud the Mighty, died in 892 A.D. after he was bitten by a man he had decapitated in battle. Siggud beheaded the man, and then mounted his head on his horse, and as he was riding off, the teeth in the head scratched his leg. It created a wound that became septic, and eventually caused his death.

454. As an infant, Daniel Kish lost both eyes because of cancer, but he now navigates because he has mastered human echo-location. This means he is able to "see" using sound echoes that bounce off objects, just like how bats do it.

455. A player-vs-player fight on the video game Eve Online called Battle B-R5RB is deemed the largest battle in the history of the Internet. It went on for twenty one hours, and it involved over 7,548 player characters.

456. The word jaguar is adopted from "yaguar," a Native American term that means one who kills with a single leap.

457. India, like lots of other countries, has a yearly holiday to celebrate children. The unique thing is that their Children's Day is precisely nine months past Valentine's Day, on November 14.

458. The fear of snakes is called ophidiophobia, and it affects one in three adults.

459. The Kroger Company made the largest strawberry shortcake in the world in 2014. It was 2073 square feet (192 square meters) in size, it weighed 21,500 pounds (9,780 kilograms), and it contained more than a ton of real strawberries, and whipped and glazed toppings.

460. In The Wizard of Oz, Oscar Zoroaster Phadrig Isaac Norman

Henkle Emmanuel Ambroise Diggs is the full name of the wizard. In the original version of the story, he says that he goes by Oz because the remainder of his initials spell out the word "Pinhead."

461. "Ancient Earth" is an interactive digital map on the Internet that can indicate to you where the ground you are currently standing on would have been on the planet at any time in the last 750 million years.

462. Grown up goat bucks usually urinate on their own beards, front legs, and even heads before they start a mating ritual.

463. Ludger Sylbaris got into a bar brawl and was placed in solitary confinement, just before a major volcanic eruption destroyed the city of Saint-Pierre. Ludger was one of just three survivors of the eruption because his cell was heavily sheltered. That prison cell still exists today.

464. National Jealousy Day is celebrated in Finland every year on November 1, and it's a holiday where everyone's taxable income is publicly revealed at eight in the morning.

465. A small number of people are born with total immunity, or some level of resistance to the AIDS causing virus, HIV. Unfortunately they only make up an estimated 1% of the population.

466. The "Wraparound" is a spider species in Australia that has the unique ability to wrap its body around small branches to conceal itself from birds and other predators.

467. When Donald Duck turned fifty in 1984, he was given a birthday parade in Disney World. The parade float included live ducks that wore party hats, and they were covered with a plexiglass barrier.

468. The biggest beaver dam to ever be discovered was found in Alberta, Canada, at the Wood Buffalo National Park. Experts claim that it has been under construction from the 1970's, and that several genera-tions of beavers have worked on it so far. It's more than 2,798 feet (eighty five meters) in length, and it's so gigantic that it's visible from space.

469. The only birds in the world that have calf muscles are the Emu birds, which are flightless and are native to Australia. They are

famous for their high endurance and speed when running over long distances. Strangely, emus cannot walk backwards, and no one understands why.

470. Matt Groening, creator of the animated series The Simpsons, told the writers of the show in a meeting in the early years, that if the character Marge ever let her hair down, people would learn for the first time that she has rabbit ears.

471. You can keep apples from browning by using lemon juice. It prevents the reaction that turns apples brown, which is between oxygen in air and polyphenol oxidase, an enzyme found in apples.

472. Bruce Buffer, the UFC announcer, and Michael Buffer, the boxing announcer, were actually long-lost half-brothers, and they had never met until they realized that they have the same biological father when they were grownups.

473. In the blockbuster movie Jurassic Park, released in 1993, the sounds of barking velociraptors were sourced by Gary Rydstrom, a sound engineer who went to Marine World and recorded the sound of mating tortoises.

474. Two Spanish brothers from Girona sold a counterfeit Francisco de Goya painting for 1.7 million Swiss Francs to someone claiming to be a Sheik in December, 2014. They later found out that the notes were photocopied, and they were just as fake as the painting.

475. The Federal Emergency Management Agency (FEMA) informally uses a scale called the Waffle House index to state the severity of an incoming storm. Waffle House is known for leaving its restaurants open despite bad weather, so, when they label a storm as "the restaurant is closed," it implies that there's imminent severe damage.

476. Newborn babies don't really shed any tears, even though they cry a lot. It's because their tear ducts aren't functional until they're between three and twelve weeks old.

477. "The Contest," an episode of the sitcom Seinfeld, was named the all-time best TV episode by TV Guide in 2009 in addition to winning an Emmy award for writing when it originally aired. The whole episode

revolved around masturbation, but the topic was never mentioned directly, and euphemisms weren't used either.

478. As a bomber flew over North Carolina in 1961 with a crew of eight, it crashed and dropped two very powerful hydrogen bomb payloads, and it killed three crew members. The two bombs dropped before the bomber hit the ground, and they didn't go off. The cleanup crew located all the remnants of the first bomb, but they weren't able to find parts of the second one.

479. President Charles King of Liberia ran for re-election in 1927, and he got 234,000 votes, although Liberia had only 15,000 registered voters at the time. King's election holds the Guinness World Record for being the most fraudulent one in history.

480. The Nazi party actually pioneered the first ever public anti-tobacco and anti-smoking movement in history, after German doctors found links between lung cancer and cigarette smoking.

481. Brian Acton failed to get a job he had applied for at Facebook in 2009, but that might be the best thing that could have happened to him. Five years after that, in 2014, Facebook bought Acton's company WhatsApp for $19 billion. From his profits, Acton took $50 million and invested it into a WhatsApp competitor called Signal. On March 20, 2018, he sent out a tweet urging everyone to delete Facebook.

482. People who have friends outlive those who don't according to studies. Having many friends is better for your health than quitting smoking, and it has double the benefits of physical activity to your life expectancy.

483. The irrational fear of clothes is called vestiphobia. People with this disorder experience tremors, difficult breathing, shortness of breath, or heart palpitations when they wear clothes, particularly tight ones.

484. Every day at five in the morning, John Quincy Adams, the sixth president of America, would swim naked in the Potomac River.

485. American scientists blew up a hydrogen bomb that was a hundred times as powerful as the one used in Hiroshima right outside the atmosphere in the summer of 1962, just to find out what would happen.

486. Caterpillars remain in the larval stage for several weeks, within which time they tend to eat more than 27,000 times their own body weight. They also expand in size several times through the molting process, and they can grow to 1,000 times their original mass. Caterpillars have about 4,000 muscles within their small bodies, and by comparison, humans only have 629.

487. In 2007, the Government of Australia spent eighty four million dollars creating a porn filter for the Internet, but a sixteen year old student at a private school in Melbourne was able to crack the code and get through that filter within thirty minutes. The boy said that the filter could be deactivated with just a few clicks.

488. According to a study, mass murderers and serial killers are born in higher numbers in November than in any other month.

489. Originally, M&M's were only sold to the US Military and it was part of soldiers' rations in wartime.

490. When trains run late in Japan, transit staff show up at the stations to apologize to commuter passengers and issue them with train delay certificates.

491. Two neuroscientists were successful in implanting a fake memory in a mouse's brain in 2012. The mouse was aghast as it remembered something that never really happened to it.

492. Nathaniel Hawthorne, the American novelist, inserted the "W" into his last name because he wanted the fact that he was related to John Hathorne, his great-great-grandfather, to remain secret. John Hathorne was a judge during the Salem Witch Trials, and is the only one who didn't repent for his actions.

493. The deepest mail box in the world is in a small Japanese fishing town called Susami, according to the Guinness Book of World Records. It's an old-school red mailbox that's located thirty two feet (ten meters) under water, and divers often place waterproof letters there and they are then collected in regular intervals. The mailbox is quite active, as it receives one to five thousand pieces of mail annually.

494. When bats are born, they come out feet first, and in many cases,

the mother bat hangs upside down so she can catch the baby in her wings as it exits the womb.

495. To win mates, male jumping spiders sing and dance. They rub together their two body segments to generate vibrations, which are essentially songs that the females hear through slits on their legs that act as ears.

496. In the mid 1990's, DC and Marvel comics had a crossover event where popular superheroes from both universes clashed. During the series, DC's Flash was challenged to a race by Quicksilver from Marvel. The Flash won the race, but was disappointed that the two speedsters couldn't be friends.

497. In the eleventh century, Vikings sailed to North America and settle there. They fished for salmon, built canoes using animal hides, and even planted wild grapes.

498. Although the cities of Nagasaki and Hiroshima were the sites of nuclear bombings, those places are no longer radioactive today because the explosion happened fairly high up in the air, and the resultant radioactive fireball never touched the land which reduced the nuclear fallout.

499. Legendary director Stephen Spielberg had been named in forty two academy Award acceptance speeches as of February, 2015, more than any other filmmaker.

500. The number of possible piece placement iterations on a chess board outnumber the number of atoms in the known universe.

501. Robert Heft submitted a design of the American flag in 1958, and then president Dwight D. Eisenhower accepted it as the official design. Heft, who was seventeen at the time, had gotten a B minus for his flag design, but his teacher changed his grade to an A after the flag was chosen by the president.

502. Daniel Boria, a twenty six year old business owner from Calgary, Canada, was arrested after he tied 120 helium balloons to his chair on July 5, 2015, and used it to float over the city. Daniel said he was trying to advertise his cleaning business. He was fined $25,000 for his stunt.

503. Kit Kat bars became a big hit in Japan partly because by sheer coincidence, "Kit Kat" sounds like "Kitto katsu," a Japanese phrase that means "you will certainly win." So people in Japan believe that this chocolate brings good luck.

504. The loud gurgling sounds produced by your stomach on occasion have a name. It's known as borborygmus, and although people think it's your body's way of telling you that you are getting hungry, it's really just your intestines shifting gases around the place.

505. The New Madrid region close to the Mississippi River in what's modern day Arkansas was hit by an earthquake on February 7, 1812, after several months of tremors. They estimated that it was an extremely powerful 8.8 magnitude earthquake that literally forced the Mississippi river to flow upstream for a little while.

506. The first cheetah race at Romford Stadium, London, was held on December 11, 1937. A female cheetah called Helen raced two greyhounds, attaining a speed of fifty five miles (eighty eight kilometers) per hour, which immediately earned her the title "Queen of the Track."

507. Pattie Boyd was married to the late Beatles band member George Harrison, and was the inspiration for the song "Something." Interestingly, she's also the inspiration for "Layla," the hit song by Eric Clapton, in which Clapton admits that he's in love with his friend's wife.

508. The Jägermeister emblem represents the Patron Saint of Hunters, Saint Hubertus, who lived in Germany in the seventh century.

509. The Chan's Megastick is the longest insect known to man. These insects are native to Borneo, Malaysia, can grow to over fourteen inches (thirty five centimeters), and they look like long twigs, which allows them to easily hide from predators.

510. The term oxymoron is in itself an oxymoron. It was coined from two ancient Greek words; "oxy" meaning sharp, "moros" meaning dull or foolish.

511. Sony BMG tried to keep its copyrighted music from being pirated from 2005 to 2007 by putting a legal rootkit on twenty two million CDs they had produced. When the discs were inserted into computers, the

rootkit software modified the computer's operating system to make copying the CD almost impossible, and users couldn't delete the program. The software also sent users' music listening habits back to Sony, so ironically, the rootkit created to prevent copyright infringement, wound up being a copyright infringement.

512. Gustav the pigeon flew 150 miles (241 kilometers) to Britain during the Second World War to inform them about the Normandy invasion, and he was awarded the Dickin Medal of Honor for his contribution.

513. If you take a close look at the Liberty Bell in Philadelphia, you'll notice that Pennsylvania is wrongly spelled, and it's missing one "N."

514. Some dolphin species are born with hair, which then falls out shortly after birth.

515. Children in Nigeria don't have as much access to cookies as those in the west, so Nigeria's version of Sesame Street has a character named Zobi the Yam Monster who is the equivalent of the Cookie Monster.

516. If you look into the sky at night, you'll be able to see five times as many meteors past midnight, than before midnight.

517. Regina Rhode had the tragic misfortune of being a student at Columbine High School during the mass shooting, and then again at Virginia Tech during a similar shooting. Luckily, she managed to avoid the shooter in both instances.

518. One of the people who translated the Dead Sea Scrolls, John M. Allegro, was certain that Christianity was based on a fertility cult and the use of psychedelic mushrooms.

519. Japanese golf players buy an odd kind of insurance that covers them in case they get a hole in one. It's a tradition there, you have to buy drinks for friends if you get a hole in one, so the insurance pays out up to $3,000 to cover that expense.

520. People who are born with lighter-colored eyes, such as green, blue, or grey, are more likely to become addicted to alcohol, according to researchers who studied the phenomenon at the University of Vermont. Those with blue eyes developed alcohol dependence at the highest rate.

521. The average distance from Earth to the moon is long enough to fit in all the planets of the solar system.

522. With average speeds of 3.54 Mbps, the Philippines is the country with the slowest Internet in the entire Southeast Asia as of 2014. In comparison, Singapore's Internet speeds average at roughly sixty-five Mbps, and it's the second fastest in the region.

523. When renowned astronaut Neil Armstrong, the first man to walk on the moon, sent his job application to NASA, it arrived a week late. Fortunately, his friend Dick Day, who also worked for NASA, managed to sneak his application in with the ones that came in on time. Were it not for his good friend Day, Armstrong would never have walked on the moon.

524. The skeletal remains of the all-time largest rodent in the world was discovered in Venezuela in 2003. It was basically a guinea pig the size of a cow. It lived eight million years ago, weighed 1,500 pounds (700 kilograms), measured 9.8 feet (three meters) long and 4.2 feet (1.3 meters) tall.

525. The largest, most extravagant hotel in Las Vegas is the MGM Grand Hotel and Casino. An estimated 15,000 pillow cases are cleaned at the hotel's laundry rooms every single day.

526. The Amazon River used to flow from east to west in prehistoric times, and not from west to east as it does today, according to studies done in 2006. In fact, for a brief period, it used to flow in both directions.

527. A bio-battery powered by sugar with ten times the power storage capacity of lithium was made by Virginia Tech researchers. This implies that cellphones could potentially run on enzymes.

528. Bees are the only animals on the planet which create food that is consumed by humans.

529. To commemorate its twentieth birthday in 1997, Apple released the TAM (Twentieth Anniversary Mac), a limited edition computer specifically marketed to executives. It cost $7,500 and it looked futuris-

tic. Apple had it hand-delivered to customers in a limo by an employee wearing a tuxedo.

530. "Ingvar Kamprad Elmtaryd Agunnaryd" is the full name from which the popular name of the Swedish furniture chain IKEA is derived. It's actually the name of the company's founder, the name of the farm in which he grew up, and the name of his hometown.

531. Although it's claimed the Leaning Tower of Pisa in Italy sank after it was constructed, the structure was never actually straight in the first place. The tower's foundation was set in soft ground, so it never settled properly, and it could never support the tower's weight evenly.

532. In Brazil, there is a stadium called "Zerao" that's positioned right over the equator. When matches are played there, technically each player is in a different hemisphere.

533. There are species of termites that are natural suicide bombers. When these termites come across a predator that endangers them and their colonies, they hold onto the enemy, then squeeze their own midsection so hard that they burst and die, while sending out sticky, hardening, or toxic substances towards the predator in all directions.

534. From two feet (sixty one centimeters) away, Bruce Lee could strike you in just 500th of a second.

535. Commanders in British Trident Submarines were told during the Cold War that if the BBC Radio 4 program "Today" was off the air for three recurring days without any explanations, they should assume that Britain had been destroyed, and act accordingly. If that happened, the commanders were to open sealed envelopes and follow the instructions outlined by the Prime Minister.

536. For people in Finland, saunas are such an integral part of life that in the Second World War, their soldiers used the logs and natural terrain to build saunas inside war zones. These saunas were only used at night time to avoid attracting the enemy.

537. Throughout Walter Summerford's life, until his death in 1912, he was struck by lightning three different times. Four years after his death, his tombstone too was struck by lightning.

538. The US government put poisonous chemicals in industrial alcohol in the Prohibition Era, hoping that it would deter people from stealing, distilling, and selling it, and that resulted in more than 10,000 deaths because the plan didn't work.

539. If you started out with one cent and you doubled your money every single day, you'd be a millionaire just twenty seven days later. You would have $1,342,177 on day twenty seven.

540. William Phelps Eno, the man who invented traffic circles, one-way streets, pedestrian safety islands, and taxi stands, never actually learned to drive because he thought that driving was a fad.

541. Although his twitter account has roughly eighteen million followers, Pope Francis has never actually been on the Internet once in his life.

542. A New York resident named Jeffrey Tanenhaus rented a commuter Citi Bike and rode it 3,000 miles (4,800 kilometers) across America in 2015. He was charged $1,200 in overtime fees, the highest for the NYC Citi Bike.

543. The lengthiest mountain range in the world is really located under the sea. It's called the Mid Ocean ridge, and it's a volcanic ridge that stretches over 49,000 miles (80,000 kilometers).

544. Because of high levels of carbon dioxide, Tasmania Island has what could be the cleanest air in the whole world.

545. People all over India worked together on July 11, 2013, to plant more trees in twenty four hours than any other group before. As part of the effort to fight climate change, they broke the world record when 800,000 volunteers showed up to take part in the activity, and they managed to plant approximately fifty million trees.

546. Britain used to have a half penny coin, until it was decommissioned in 1984.

547. The rings around planet Saturn have a circumference of roughly 500,000 miles (805,000 kilometers), but they are only about one foot (thirty centimeters) thick.

548. If you take the total number of people bitten by sharks in the

whole world in a year, and then multiply it by ten, you'll end up with the approximate number of people who are bitten by other people, just in New York alone.

549. Mars Needs Moms, an animated motion picture film from Disney, cost $150 million to produce, but it only made $6.9 million when it debuted domestically at the box office. Its opening was the 12th worst of all time.

550. When you are deep in sleep, you burn more calories than you do when you are sitting on a sofa and watching TV.

551. Domestic cats, bottlenose dolphins, and some other carnivorous animals are unable to taste or even detect sugar or any sweetness because of a genetic mutation.

552. A West African chimpanzee named Washoe was the first non-human to grasp American Sign Language. She was able to learn just like human infants, by observing and imitating people.

553. When making Spiderman Homecoming, the 2017 Marvel block-buster, Tom Holland was trolled by Michael Keaton, who kept quoting lines from his movie, The Dark Knight. In one specific fight scene, as Spiderman (Holland) punched Vulture (Keaton), Keaton turned around and whispered "I'm Batman" in a dark tone, which threw off Holland.

554. A six acre island in Maine was purchased by the makers of Cards against Humanity, a popular game, and they renamed it "Hawaii II" because it is in the mainland.

555. Squids can shoot out water so fast that the squirt can propel them through the air at a speed of up to twenty five miles (forty kilometers) per hour.

556. To protect the royal lineage in the event of a plane crash, two heirs to the throne aren't supposed to travel together on the same plane. This tradition was broken by Prince William, who took his son Prince George to Australia on the same flight when the little prince was nine months old.

557. When filming "The Hunger Games: Mockingjay," according to

Liam Hemsworth, fellow actor Jennifer Lawrence would intentionally eat something gross, like tuna or garlic, whenever the two had to kiss.

558. Have you ever heard a catchy song, and then, after that, it got stuck in your head, replaying itself over and over again? There's an actual name for such songs. They are called "earworms."

559. Thomas Jefferson purchased a new thermometer several days before he signed the Declaration of Independence on July 4, 1776. He used it to record the temperature in Philadelphia, Pennsylvania, on the historical day, and it was seventy six degrees Fahrenheit (or twenty four degrees Celsius) when the document was signed.

560. The Manhattan skyline has grown by more than 300 meters in the past one hundred years, and it still continues to grow as more buildings have been planned.

561. With your eyes closed, you can still touch your nose because of proprioception, a sense beyond the basic five ones that you know about. It's an extra meta-sense that enables you to feel the positions of your body parts relative to each other.

562. In an effort to prove that the Earth was hollow, John Quincy Adams, during his tenure as US President, began an expedition to the center of the Earth.

563. The Simpsons character Krusty the Clown was originally supposed to be Homer disguising himself in a clown costume, the inside joke being that Bart loved Krusty but hated Homer.

564. Several people who hiked in the Tomoka Riverside woods close to Daytona, Florida, between 1955 and 1966 reported seeing a strange pink-colored fog that seemed to stay near the ground. Lots of these people believe the fog was carnivorous, and they blame it for the disappearances of about twelve different people. To date, no one knows what the fog was, or where it originated from.

565. An American congressman named Andrew May remarked during a press conference in June, 1943, that American submarines were able to survive Japanese attacks because the enemy was setting depth charges at shallow depths. The Japanese heard his comment and started modi-

fying their depth charges, and this resulted in the loss of 800 American lives.

566. Neil Evenhuis discovered an extinct type of fly which he named Carmenelectra Shechisme after Carmen Electra, the model and actress, and he published his findings in 2002.

567. Scatomancy involves telling a person's fortune by examining their poop, and it's a practice that has existed for thousands of years. Fortune tellers who do this are known as scatomancers.

568. To bring attention to the issue of unequal pay, a brief episode of Batman was made in 1973, starring Adam West. Robin and Batman were tied up close to a time bomb, and Batgirl, played by Yvonne Craig, came in and stated that it was too late, and that she made less money than Robin did, which wasn't right, or in accordance with the Federal Equal Pay Law.

569. There's a condition called white coat syndrome that affects 20% of patients, and it involves the dramatic rise in their blood pressure when they are in a doctor's office.

570. The name Jessica was the number one name for baby-girls in America for several years in the 1980's and 1990's, but did you know that it was really created by William Shakespeare? He made it up for his play, "The Merchant of Venice." He is also credited with coining popular phrases such as "vanish into thin air, bated breath, dead as a doornail," and "kill with kindness."

571. The Center for Disease Control and Prevention estimates that in 2014, smokeless tobacco and cigarette companies pumped nine billion dollars into advertising and promoting their products just in the United States alone.

572. Instead of using periscope controllers in their submarines, the US Navy is now using Xbox 360 controllers, and that has cut the training time for operators from several hours to only a few minutes.

573. Balls made of steel or solid glass can bounce higher than ordinary non-bouncy balls made of rubber if they are dropped from the same

height. That's because the harder balls don't lose much energy when they impact the floor.

574. In Las Vegas, it's illegal to pawn your dentures because they are considered under the law as prescribed medical devices.

575. The Guava is a super fruit. It has four times the Vitamin C in an orange, more potassium than a standard banana, and compared to pineapples, it has four times the fiber and three times the protein.

576. "Noix de Vie," which translates to "nuts of life," is a mouse-sized French shop located on the side of a building in Malmo, Sweden. Right next to it is a similarly-sized Italian restaurant Il Topolino, which means "Mickey Mouse." They were both built into the wall of a building by an artist called Anonymouse.

577. The Dragon Bridge is a steel bridge in Vietnam. It has the shape of the mythical creature, and it includes a head which shoots out jets of water, and fireballs.

578. A Taliban commander named Mohammed Ashan turned himself in at a checkpoint operated by Afgan soldiers in April, 2012, hoping to claim the one hundred dollar reward they had offered for his capture. He didn't get his reward, but he was arrested.

579. Jack Black got addicted to cocaine when he was fourteen following his parents' divorce. Thankfully, he got sober after seeing a therapist at Poseidon, a Los Angeles school for troubled teens.

580. The Powerpuff Girls, the animated girl superheroes, were originally created by Craig McCracken as a college project. At the time the project was named "Whoopass Stew."

581. Dog collars that have studs and spikes are used for decorative purposes these days, but originally, these dog collars were used by shepherds who put them around dogs' necks in Turkey years ago, to protect the dogs from wolves.

582. McDonald's was nicknamed "Macca's" in Australia. In 2013, this name became so popular, that it was changed officially, including on signs.

583. Ed O'Neill, best known for his acting roles on Modern Family and Married with Children, is a black belt Brazilian Jiu Jitsu fighter. He got his black-belt in 2007, and he has more than twenty two years of practice in the martial art.

584. Originally, golfer Tiger Woods was named Eldrick Tonk Woods. In his early golfing days, a few reporters started calling him Eldrick "Tiger" Woods. After gaining fame, he ditched the name Eldrick.

585. President Gerald Ford's seventeen year old daughter Susan Ford hosted her high school prom on May 31, 1975, at the White House. The senior prom for Holton-Arms School turned out to be the only one ever to take place at the presidential mansion.

586. Certain words have been altered overtime due to metathesis, which refers to the swapping of sounds. For instance, bird used to be "brid," wasp was "waps" and horse was "hros."

587. A homeless man called Leo Grand met a programmer called Patrick McConlogue who asked him to choose between a hundred dollars and sixteen coding lessons back in 2013. Leo took the coding lessons, and he ended up creating an app called "Trees for Cars." The app aims to reduce carbon dioxide emissions by lowering the number of cars in traffic through carpooling.

588. Stomach acid has a pH range of one to three, which means it's extremely strong. It has a similar approximate strength to battery acid. A single drop of stomach acid can corrode through a piece of wood.

589. Renowned gangster Al Capone left prison in 1939 after which he was treated for paresis at Union Memorial Hospital for some time. When he was discharged, Capone gave two weeping cherry trees to the hospital as a sign of appreciation.

590. The highest temperature officially recorded on Earth was 134 degrees Fahrenheit (56.7 degrees Celsius). It happened July 10, 1913, in Death Valley, California, at the Greenland Ranch. The coldest recorded temperature was negative 135.8 degrees Fahrenheit (negative 94.7 degrees Celsius), according to data from NASA satellites. It occurred in Antarctica in August, 2010.

591. A walrus can stay up for eighty-four hours without having to sleep.

592. Times Square had a waterfall back in 1948 that was known as the Bond Waterfall. It had a height of twenty six feet (eight meters), a length of 131 feet (forty meters) and was designed to flow at a rate of 8,350 gallons (38,000 liters) per minute.

593. Muammar Gaddafi was really the richest man in the world before the Libyan National Transitional Council ousted and executed him on October 20, 2011. He was worth north of $200 billion if you consider his bank accounts, corporate investments around the world, and other assets.

594. The Berlin Holocaust Memorial Project had to be stopped in 2003, after it was discovered that the company contracted to make a coating that would prevent graffiti on the monument was the same exact company that was contracted to manufacture the gas used to murder millions of Jews in concentration camps during the Second World War.

595. In Salt Lake City, University of Utah researchers found a correlation between the size of people's utensils, and how much food they consumed. The bottom-line is that the bigger your fork, the less you eat.

596. Two million out of the twenty one million cases of diabetes that are projected to develop in America by 2020 might be prevented if people quit taking drinks with artificial sweeteners, according to a study done by Cambridge University researchers in 2015.

597. In order to understand and cure diseases more effectively, scientists in Japan successfully designed and bred fluorescent monkeys. The researchers however received a lot of backlash from various ethical groups who didn't approve of their experiments.

598. The United States nuclear weapons system is very much out of date, and it still runs on floppy disks, which were last popular in the 1980's, according to a Government Accountability Office Report.

599. The thagomizer refers to the group of four to ten spikes on tails of specific dinosaurs known as stegosauri. It's believed that these spikes were a defense mechanism against predators.

600. Damselflies and dragonflies have a mating ritual where they form their bodies into a heart shape. The claspers at the end of the male's abdomen fit into the grooves on the female one of the same species, and they both bend until they form a heart shape.

601. If by some tragedy you lose a thumb or finger and a doctor isn't there to save it on time, you can actually replace it by transplanting a toe in its place, in a procedure known as toe-to-hand transplant.

602. The left hand is unclean according to Indian culture because it's used to wipe the bottom, while the right hand is used to greet others and eat food. When in India, only use your right hand to greet people, receive items, and exchange cash.

603. Wax worms are newly discovered types of worms that can eat and process polyethylene, the plastic material in shopping bags. Polyethylene makes up 40% of plastics used within Europe, and scientists are hoping wax worms could be used to break down plastic bags that are polluting waterways and overwhelming landfills.

604. When people get kidney transplants, surgeons don't usually take out the defective organ. They just add the third one into the body.

605. The Giant African Land Snails are as big as rats. They can chew through materials such as plaster, and if you drive over one, its shell is strong enough to puncture your tires. They can grow to 7.9 inches (twenty centimeters), live for about nine years, and produce about 1,200 eggs every year.

606. In Indiana prisons, they give death row inmates their meal of choice two or three days prior to execution, because most of them are rarely hungry on the day they know they'll die.

607. More Americans voted during the fifth season finale of American Idol than during the 1984 election in which Ronald Reagan won the presidency. There were 54.5 million votes cast during the election, compared to sixty three million for the TV show.

608. The tumbleweed is seen as a symbol of desolation in the American West, but it doesn't actually originate from America. It's a flowering plant called "kali tragus" that's native to Russia, and it first grew in

South Dakota in 1879 after its seeds were accidentally mixed with imported flax seeds.

609. Planes don't crash as often as you might imagine. Very few planes ever crash, and when they do, the chances of you dying are about one in eleven million. If you are in a plane and it literally goes down, 95.7% of people in it will likely survive.

610. A vat holding 161,000 gallons (610,000 liters) of beer busted in October 17, 1814, and that caused other nearby vats of beer to rupture as well. As a result, more than 388,000 gallons (1,470,000 liters) of beer flooded the streets, and eight people drowned.

611. The Florida city of Key West was frustrated that it was being treated as a foreign country with border patrol blocks everywhere, so on April 23, 1982, it seceded from the United States, becoming a conch republic. The newly created country then declared war on America, surrendered in less than a minute, and then applied for a billion dollars of foreign aid almost immediately. Interestingly, the strange plan worked, and they soon removed the annoying roadblocks from the city.

612. Lin Ching Lan, a choreographer and dancer from Taiwan, was born deaf, so she feels the vibrations in her feet which come from wooden floors when music plays, and uses it to get her rhythm. She founded a dance troop for the hearing impaired, and she has appeared in a few commercials.

613. Hawaii was trying to control the rat population in sugarcane plantations, so they set mongooses loose in the fields in 1883. The mongooses didn't solve the problems, because it turns out they are diurnal while rats are nocturnal. Farmers soon realized both animals were a problem, and the population of native birds has drastically fallen since then.

614. Rage Yoga is an actual yoga class that's offered in Calgary, at the Dickens Pub. Participants perform traditional yoga poses which are combined with heavy metal rock, as people scream vulgarities and make lewd gestures such as the middle finger.

615. Students in Sweden are literally paid by the government to go to

school. Students between the ages of sixteen and twenty are paid a monthly salary that ranges from $570 to $693.

616. Edinburgh Castle, which is the most popular paid tourist attraction in Scotland, was originally constructed on top of a volcano plug. The plug is named Castle Rock, and is 350 million years old.

617. If you ignore the diseases transmitted by mosquitoes, it would take roughly 400,000 mosquitoes to draw enough blood from a person for it to result in death, and it would require a million mosquitoes to drain all the blood from an average sized person's body.

618. Twenty four children ages seven to twelve were able to recognize their own mother's voice in under a second 97% of the time, even when the mom spoke in pure gibberish, according to a study done by the Stanford University School of Medicine.

619. Hollywood visionary Stuart Freeborn made Yoda for the movie "Star Wars Episode Five: The Empire Strikes Back," by modeling the sage green Jedi master's character from a composite of his own face and that of scientist Albert Einstein.

620. Electric blue fire streams down from the peak of Indonesia's Kawah Ijen Volcano during the night. Sulphur-based gases burn at the volcano, causing the glow.

621. The laser doesn't actually take the ink away when it's used to remove tattoos. It merely breaks down the ink, so that your body can flush it out. So your tattoo technically leaves your body when you go to the toilet.

622. A philosopher named "Democritus" discovered the existence of atoms with spaces between them, way back in 400 B.C.

623. Several researchers have come to the conclusion that Maurice Hilleman, an American doctor, saved more lives in the twentieth century than any other scientists. The reason is because he's created about nine of the fourteen vaccines that are usually given to children, including the chicken pox, measles, and mumps vaccines.

624. The killing of sharks for their fins has reduced by 50% thanks to

conservation campaigns led by Yao Ming, the retired NBA star. Various surveys have shown that in China, 91% of people currently support the ban on consumption of shark fins.

625. Scientists officially refer to hooved mammals as ungulates.

626. You can buy a wide selection of wigs for your dog from vending machines in Tokyo, Japan. Dog wigs are so popular there that they now offer a large selection in online stores as well.

627. Satoshi Kanazawa, a research psychologist, studied over twenty thousand students for five years, and he established that night owls – those who preferred to sleep and wake up late – tend to be smarter than early risers. A different study showed that despite what early risers believe, night owls actually use their time in a productive manner. They stay mentally sharp for longer than early risers.

628. After sheep are sheared, they no longer recognize each other. At times, they fight each other as if they've never met before.

629. At just twelve years old, Calvin Graham was the youngest American serviceman in the Second World War. He received the Bronze Star, and Purple Heart medals, and in 1978, he was honorably discharged. He passed away in 1992 at age sixty two.

630. Your cheeks turn red when you blush, and the exact same thing happens to your stomach. Blushing causes capillaries all over the body to widen for higher blood flow, and because capillaries are near the surface, it causes red coloration. Blushing is just more noticeable on the cheeks than the stomach.

631. Individuals who literally hate everything and everyone are known as miso maniacs. The hate comes from the fear that everyone already hates them, so they are merely reciprocating.

632. It's alleged that Alexander the Great, Napoleon, Hitler, and Mussolini suffered from ailurophobia, which is the fear of cats.

633. During the Boshin War, a female soldier called Nakano Takeko didn't want enemy soldiers to take her head as a trophy, so her dying wish was for her sister to chop it off and bury it.

634. The Carolingian Community in Kenya only makes up 0.06% of the human population, but it has produced about 70% of all elite long distance running medalists. During the Berlin Marathon in 2013, male Kenyan runners won first, second, fourth, and fifth place, while female Kenyan runners won first, second, and fourth place.

635. Employees at a South Carolina 3M plant in 1980 were startled to find out that spools of plastic film that they used to manufacture stationery, had created a static electricity force-field. The employees were frozen in place, and were unable to get close to the machinery. They had to walk backwards to a space where the effects were less serious in order to get away.

636. California's wildfire firefighting personnel consist of fifty to 80% inmates, and they are paid less than two dollars an hour.

637. When hummingbirds breed, they build their nests near hawks' nests, because the hawks, which are larger and stronger, will instinctively protect the eggs from other animals.

638. "Embrotherment" was a legal classification in the Middle Ages where two men were allowed to pool their resources, move in together, and basically live like a real married couple.

639. Sir Hugh Beaver, managing director of Guinness Brewery, unsuccessfully shot at a golden plover in 1951, and subsequently got into a debate on whether the bird was the fastest of all European game birds. He realized that there was no resource he could reference to settle the argument, so he made his own resource, and so the Guinness Book of World Records was born.

640. Nobel Laureate William Shockley, who's credited with inventing the transistor, once argued that individuals with IQs under a hundred should be paid and then willingly sterilized.

641. Squids have an esophagus that passes through their brain, which is shaped like a donut, and this means that if they swallow large objects, it could literally result in brain damage.

642. Urine produced by the maned wolf has the exact same smell as

marijuana. That's because both the animal's urine and the plant contain pyrazine, which gives them their characteristic smell.

643. Bjorn De La Cruz, who co-owns the Brooklyn based Manila Social Club and is an executive chef there, created a gold-dusted twenty-four karat doughnut that's served with Cristal Champagne and costs $100.

644. After Disney wrapped up the show "Boy Missed World," they forbade the cast from taking any keepsakes, but Rider Strong whose character was Shawn Hunter stole his leather jacket from the set. He later left the jacket in a parked car in NYC and it was stolen.

645. On average, every motorists spends more than two days per year in traffic, just waiting for the light to turn from red to green.

646. Cannabinoids are a group of chemicals usually found in cannabis plants, but they are only present in two other places; in chocolate and in the human brain.

647. After it's used for ten years, the average mattress will double in weight because it accumulates dead skin, dust mites, and sweat.

648. A bird dropped a baguette on the large Hadron Collider in 2009, and it is blamed for causing a technical fault.

649. 95% of all people in Suriname live along the country's northern coast. That's because 91% of the whole country is a dense jungle.

650. A team of Japanese researchers at Keio University in Tokyo, successfully taught pigeons to differentiate between Monet and Picasso paintings in the early 1990's. After seeing several works from both artists, the birds could recognize other pieces by the artists, which they have never actually seen before.

651. A super pack of 400 wolves started to attack the village of Vircoyans in Russia in 2011, and within four days, they had killed thirty horses. Local authorities sent out parties of hunters, and they consulted experts who were all mystified as to why the wolves had created such a large pack.

652. You have a magnetic bone within your head right now. It's located above your nose where some think your third eye is situated, and it's

called the ethmoid bone. Because it's magnetic, it aids your sense of direction.

653. In the 1960's, Columbia University researchers conducted an experiment called the "Smoke-Filled Room," in which students were put in rooms and asked to fill forms while smoke was pumped inside through vents. Students who were alone almost invariably left the room to report the smoke. Strangely, when the students were joined in the room by actors who pretended not to notice the smoke, only one out of ten of them went to report the smoke. Most of the others kept trying to fill their forms, as they occasionally waved the smoke away.

654. Writer's cramp is the term for when you get muscular spasms in your forefingers and thumb, but the medical term for the phenomenon is called graphospasm.

655. You can distinguish between identical twins by looking at their belly buttons. Navels aren't genetic, they are scars that are left behind when the umbilical cord is removed.

656. The City of Jericho, located in modern day Palestinian territory, is the oldest city in the world, and it dates back 10,000 years.

657. The state of Virginia has a law that allows people to legally hunt raccoons on Sunday, provided that it's all done before 2:00 A.M.

658. The god of smallpox is named Sopona, and was worshipped in Nigeria, until it was outlawed after media reports indicated that a cult was intentionally spreading the disease to make the god more powerful.

659. Twyndyllyngs is the longest English word that has no vowels, and it means twinlings, or twins.

660. Ambrosia is a startup based in Monterey, California, that infuses clients with blood plasma from young adults or teenagers to slow down aging.

661. Most foods don't taste too good on airplanes because when you fly, your taste buds along with your sense of smell are impacted. When in a pressurized cabin, your perception of sweetness and saltiness naturally reduces.

662. The largest gingerbread house in the world was created in 2013 in Bryan, Texas, according to the Guinness World Records. It was fifty nine feet (eighteen meters) long, thirty nine feet (twelve meters) wide and nine feet (three meters) high. The entire house was edible, and in total, all baking ingredients used made up over thirty five million calories.

663. Your kidneys receive approximately 25% of all the blood in your heart.

664. Elvis Presley was figuring out plans for his first European tour when he died. Outside the United States, he only held five music events, and they were all in Canada.

665. H2NO was an upselling campaign that was once launched by Coca-Cola, the soft drink giant. The campaign has a website that trained waiters to talk customers into buying sodas instead of asking for free water.

666. Ellen DeGeneres was asked to play Phoebe in the show Friends, but she declined before Lisa Kudrow was cast for the part.

667. Originally released in 1993, the hit song "Whoomp, there it is" still makes about $500,000 annually. It has been called both the best and worst song of the 1990's.

668. 17,000 people from twenty eight developed western nations participated in a survey that found that live-in boyfriends on average did more housework than married men. It also found that married women did more chores than live-in girlfriends.

669. Velociraptors are portrayed as larger than humans in the Jurassic Park film franchise, but the fact is that they were really the size of domestic turkeys, and it's possible that they even had feathers.

670. It's considered illegal to wear a bullet resistant vest in New Jersey when committing a violent crime.

671. The nictitating membrane is a third eyelid that dogs have, and according to Deborah Friedman of the American College of Veterinary Ophthalmologists, the membrane has four functions. Firstly, it cleans debris from the dog's eyes. Secondly, it produces one third of the dog's

tears. Thirdly, it helps fight off infections; and lastly, it prevents injury to the eye.

672. One of the most popular Marvel Comic heroes, Wolverine, is only five feet two inches (1.57 meters) tall, but he weighs 300 pounds (136 kilos) because of the adamantium in his skeletal system.

673. Singer Frank Sinatra couldn't get ringside tickets to the Mohammed Ali vs. Joe Fraser fight, which was then billed as the fight of the century, so the singer struck a deal with Life Magazine to work as their photographer, and he got his ringside seat, right in the press box. He took pictures of the fight, and four of them were used in the magazine, including one that was on the cover.

674. It's estimated that the asteroid that impacted the Earth and killed the dinosaurs about sixty six million years ago would have hit thirteen on the Richter scale that's used to rate earthquakes. Anything that hits fifteen on that scale would totally destroy the planet.

675. Pingu, the Swiss Claymation children's TV character, doesn't just speak gibberish, he actually speaks a specific nonsense language called Grammelot. The language has been around since the sixteenth century, and was used by clowns in theaters.

676. Studies show that people notice your shoes or whatever you are wearing on your feet on a subconscious level before they notice anything else about you.

677. In the video game Super Mario Bros that was made for the first Nintendo Entertainment System, the white clouds above and the green bushes below were basically the same, they were just colored differently.

678. Legendary Artist Vincent Van Gogh made the majority of his paintings from May, 1889 to May, 1890, during which time he had checked himself into a mental institution in Saint-Remy-de-Provence, France, called Saint Paul Asylum.

679. Research done in London shows that over a million lives could be saved each year if everyone in the world washed their hands properly.

680. Water doesn't conduct electricity very well. In fact, it's really an

insulator. Water only conducts electricity because of the impurities in it, and not the water molecules themselves.

681. Between 1932 and 1939, Oskar Speck, a twenty five year old Canoeist from Germany, paddled a folding kayak from his home country to Australia just to see the world. He covered more than 31,000 miles (50,000 kilometers).

682. Data from the American Veterans Affairs Department shows that out of one hundred people, about seven or eight of them will suffer from post-traumatic stress disorder at least once in their lives. Currently, eight million grownups have PTSD.

683. Obesity has the same effects in parrots as it does in humans. Even worse, parrots with obesity are likely to get cancer.

684. When the popular song "Take Me Out to the Ball Game" was written by Albert Von Tizler and Jack Norworth in 1908, neither of them had ever been to an actual baseball game.

685. The North American continent shares the same tectonic plate with half of Japan.

686. Doctor Roswell Park was called on as he performed surgery on September 6, 1901. He said he couldn't leave, not even for the president of the United States himself. Strangely, it was President William McKinley who needed his help because he had been shot, but Doctor Park still wouldn't leave surgery. President McKinley died, and a couple of weeks later, Dr. Park saved a woman who came in with injuries similar to the president's.

687. A bowl of dry corn flakes contains about 25,000 more genes than the whole human body. At the same time, humans have over 1,700 more genes than earthworms.

688. On February 11, 1964, the Beatles performed at the Washington Coliseum in the United States. The son of venue owner Harry Lynn claims that the building had a strong urine smell that night because some ladies who attended the concert wet themselves because they were so crazy about seeing the Beatles.

689. To raise funds for Glide, an organization that fights poverty, they did an eBay auction where the winner would have lunch with legendary billionaire investor Warren Buffett. Bidding started at just $25,000 and it closed at $3.3 million.

690. Katie and Amy Jones-Elliot are twins, but they were born eighty seven days apart. Their mom Maria went into labor on June 1, 2012, when she was only twenty three weeks pregnant, and she birthed Amy. Thirteen weeks later on August 27, her doctors induced labor, and she gave birth to Katie. The twins hold the world record for the longest time between the births of two twins.

691. In an extinct Australian language called Mbabarom, the word for dog was dog, and it's pronounced just like we do in English. The strange thing about this is that the language was not related to English in any way.

692. Benjamin Franklin penned an essay called "A Letter to a Royal Academy" in 1781 as he lived in France as America's Ambassador there, and it was about farting. The essay is more commonly known as "Fart Proudly," and it was his way of expressing his disapproval of how pretentious Academic Societies in Europe had become.

693. Sometimes, non-threatening lumps may form in the armpits of breastfeeding women. It happens when the breast glands are so full with milk that some of it overflows to the surrounding areas.

694. From 1946 to 1958, America blew up at least twenty three nuclear bombs at seven different test sites in the vicinity of Bikini Atoll, one of the Marshall Islands. As a result, Bikini Atoll took up a new flag in 1987, one that looked like the American flag but with five black stars in place of the white stripes. Three stars symbolized the islands destroyed by the bombs, and the other two represent the two islands currently occupied by Bikini natives, Ejit and Kili islands. The flag signifies a great debt, which Bikini maintains that it's still owed by America.

695. More than 95% of humans have a natural immunity to leprosy.

696. After terrorist attacks in the US on September 11, 2001, all flights were grounded, except for a single plane that was going to save a

person's life. The plane traveled from San Diego, California, to Miami, Florida, transporting an antivenom for a life threatening snake bite that the man had gotten. The flight was escorted by two fighter jets, and the man's life was saved.

697. "High School Musical," the successful Disney movie, started out as a 1999 script with the title "Grease Three." The idea was for Justin Timberlake and Britney Spears to have leading roles as the children of Sandy Olsson and Danny Zuko from the 1978 film Grease.

698. The highest priced beef in the world is Wagyu beef. It's priced at $50 per 3.5 ounces (a hundred grams) of the meat itself, but a rib steak will set you back $3,200.

699. Howler monkeys can be heard up to three miles (five kilometers) away when a group lets loose with their howling.

700. Actress Carrie Mulligan and singer Marcus Mumford of Mumford & Sons were childhood pen pals who lost contact. Each of them found fame on their own and both were reintroduced to each other as adults, falling in love and eventually getting married.

701. In the 1980's, it was actually possible to call 1-900-909-FRED to have Freddy Kruger of Nightmare on Elm Street tell you scary stories.

702. Stanford University has conducted clinical studies that show that people who experience auditory hallucinations, like schizophrenia, hear voices that are shaped by cultural influences. In Africa and India, voices are described to belong to family members or spirits, while in America, people describe voices as violent, torturous, and hateful yelling from strangers.

703. The last state in the United States to lift the ban on interracial marriages was Alabama, in 2000, over thirty years after the Supreme Court ruled that such a ban was unconstitutional.

704. The fastest land mammal in the United Kingdom is the European hare. They are able to reach speeds over forty four miles (seventy two kilometers) per hour.

705. Territorio De Zaguates, meaning land of the strays, is a territory in

Costa Rica where you can hike for free with dogs. It is basically a huge no-kill dog shelter.

706. Until 2011, beer was not considered an alcohol in Russia. It was in fact classified as a soft drink because it had less than 10% alcohol, so it could be bought by anybody from street kiosks, at railway stations, or at twenty four hour corner shops, just like any fruit juice or mineral water.

707. A hoglet is the name given to a baby hedgehog.

708. Female pandas generally give birth to a single cub. If she ends up having two cubs, she will take care of one and abandon the other.

709. Scientists are developing flexible electronic skin for prosthetic limbs that can help replicate the sensory capabilities of real skin, including feeling temperature changes.

710. The main source of Vitamin C for the Inuit people is found in narwhal (a type of whale) skin. In fact, there is as much Vitamin C gram for gram in narwhal skin as there is in an orange.

711. It's a tradition to eat something called Kivia at Christmas time in Iceland. The dish is made from the raw flesh of little auks, a type of Arctic bird. The birds are previously buried whole in seal skin for several months until they have reached an advanced stage of decomposition.

712. People over fifty who suffer from diabetes are given medals in the United Kingdom for their courage and perseverance of living with diabetes.

713. In 1978, a US Navy ship known as the U.S.S. Stein was found to have traces of an unknown species of giant squid attack. Almost all cuts on the sonar dome contained remains of a sharp, curved claw that were found on the rims of the suction cups of some squid tentacles, but some of the claw marks were much bigger than that of any discovered squid species.

714. The origin of the mortar used in the construction of the great pyramids of Giza is still unknown. The material has been analyzed several times and although the chemical composition is known, it cannot be reproduced. It is stronger than stone, and is why it's still

holding up today. The pyramids were built sometime between 2540 and 2560 B.C.

715. According to the Guinness World Records, on March 30, 2003, a 2.3 feet (seventy centimeter) round, ten pound (4.5 kilograms) coconut was husked by Siddaraju Raju, from Bangalore, India, using only his teeth.

716. Most meteors are the size of a grain of sand and disintegrate in the air. The larger ones that actually reach the Earth are called meteorites and they are very rare.

717. The most abundant star in the universe is the red dwarf star, which is much smaller than the sun, but has a much longer lifetime. Their surface temperatures can reach 5,846 degrees Fahrenheit (3,230 degrees Celsius).

718. In order to shred their tails, most species of geckos actually have to have their tails pulled. However, a number of species are able to get rid of their tails at will. In several cases, the tails grow back, but they no longer have the original bone structure and are made of just cartilage.

719. The letter "J" is the only letter of the alphabet that doesn't appear on the Periodic Table.

720. In preparation for the 2008 Olympics in Beijing, 1.5 million people were evicted from their homes.

721. A sixteen year old student in Ohio won an essay contest for the question "what to do with Hitler after the war" with one sentence which was: "Put him in black skin and let him live the rest of his life in America."

722. In Japan, a daruma doll or gold doll is a handmade wishing doll that keeps you focused on your goals in five steps. Step one is you establish a particular goal. Step two is you draw one on daruma's blank eyes to signify your commitment, and then write down your goal on the heart painted on the back of the doll for extra commitment. Step three is you place daruma somewhere that is visible in your home or office to remind you to stay focused on your goal. Step four, once you've achieved your goal, draw in daruma's other eye to say thank you. And step five,

write the goal you achieved on the back of the doll if you didn't, of course, already in step two. If having a new goal, then you get a new daruma doll, and repeat the process again.

723. In 1818, treadmills were created with the aim of punishing English inmates.

724. The University of Wisconsin Green Bay is using Snapchat to inform the students that they have been accepted at the university.

725. During World War II, Japan launched balloons with bombs into the jet stream. Five picnickers found one of these balloons and attempted to move it; the bomb went off and killed them. This is known as the only mainland attack in the US. The locations of many of the balloons are still unknown.

726. Thurl Ravenscroft was not only the voice of Kellogg's Tony the Tiger, but the one who sang "You're a mean one, Mr. Grinch" in the original How the Grinch Stole Christmas movie.

727. The UK based company Gumdrop recycles gum into bins and the they're made out of entirely recycled gum.

728. The popemobile is the vehicle used by the pope at public appearances. It has bulletproof glass as well as a handrail for him to hold on to while he stands and waves at the crowd in order to get in and out. It was designed to protect him and be visible at the same time.

729. After the Patriots won the Super Bowl 51, NFL player Tom Brady became the first player ever to win four Super Bowl Most Valuable Player awards.

730. Cockroaches have their own personalities and even display different character traits according to researchers from the Université Libre de Bruxelles. Although they are simple animals, they can make complex decisions on survival. One cockroach's decision can even influence others.

731. George Hotz was the first person to unlock a first-generation iPhone; he was only seventeen years old when he did so. He sold the iPhone for a Nissan 350Z and three locked phones.

732. Steve Jobs' GPA was 2.65 when in high school.

733. In one ounce of blood there are approximately 150 billion red blood cells, while in one pint of blood there are 2.4 trillion red blood cells. In fact, under stress, the human body can produce 119 million red blood cells per second.

734. In China, there's a delicacy called "Virgin Boy Eggs," where the eggs are actually soaked in the urine of boys under the age of ten. The urine is collected from school washrooms and it's strongly believed that eating this can have health benefits. It's possible to buy one for only twenty four cents.

735. A man from Bruceville, Indiana, named Bonny Ver built two roller coasters in his backyard. He named them the blue flash and he built them for his grandchildren with no prior experience, using scrap metal that he collected that he then welded together.

736. The shortest war in history was the Anglo-Zanzibar War, which only lasted thirty eight minutes.

737. Numi is a type of toilet made by Kohler, which has a heated seat, foot warmers, lights, and Bluetooth technology.

738. "NineBot" is a Chinese Segway rip-off company that used the money that it got from selling rip-off Segways to buy the original Segway Company.

739. Numerous research papers have shown that coffee can prevent cancer, reduce the chance of getting diabetes, and improve your overall health.

740. Kim Kardashian's emoji app was making $1,000,000 a minute at one point after its launch.

741. There is a white oak tree in Athens, Georgia, that legally owns itself, and eight feet of land surrounding it. According to newspapers, a deed written by Colonel William Jackson was written to the tree, giving ownership of the land to itself in the 1800's.

742. Queen termites have a really long lifespan. They can live up to fifty

years long and are the oldest ones in the colony. They can also produce eggs for up to ten years.

743. Shishito Pepper is a well-known pepper grown in Japan. Only one out of every ten is spicy, but there is no way to know which one is spicy beforehand.

744. Robert De Niro was considered an extreme actor for his time because he learned to box for the movie "Raging Bull" and actually got a taxi license for his role in the movie "Taxi Driver."

745. In Sweden, there is a hotel called the "Jumbo Stay," which has been converted from a 747 jumbo jet. It has thirty three rooms that are sixty four square feet (six square meters) wide and ten feet (three meters) from floor to ceiling, equipped with flat screen TV's, access to Wi-Fi, and private or shared showers and toilets in the corridor.

746. The Witwatersrand Basin in South Africa, which is 2.7 square miles (4.3 square kilometers) deep, has produced more gold than any other continent. About 50,000 tons have been extracted over a course of 120 years, which is nearly half the gold ever mined.

747. While building the Hoover Dam, ninety six people in total died from industrial fatalities which included drowning, blasting, falling rocks or rockslides, falls from the canyon wall, and truck accidents.

748. Before Saladin, the first Sultan of Egypt, died in 1193, he had given all of his fortune to the poor, so by the time he died, his final wealth consisted only of a single piece of gold and forty pieces of silver, not even enough to pay for the funeral.

749. The most weight of all the toes on your foot is carried by your big toe, bearing nearly 40% of your total body's weight.

750. The song "Gangsta's Paradise" by Coolio is one of their few songs to not feature any profane words because it was the only way that Stevie Wonder would authorize the sampling of his song Pastime Paradise.

751. A red card was once given just after three seconds of a football match commencing when a player yelled "Eff me, that was loud," when the whistle was blown.

752. A woman named Lina Poulsen from Sweden found her wedding ring sixteen years after she lost it, growing on a carrot in her garden.

753. In 1958, a man named Robert Lane from New York City named his son Winner and, later, another son Loser. Winner ended up as a criminal with a long prison record. Loser on the contrary, went on to prep school on a scholarship, graduated from college, and joined the New York Police Department.

754. The letter "T" was the first letter Vanna White ever turned on the game show Wheel of Fortune.

755. In Norway, it's illegal to neuter your dog, except in extreme circumstances. They believe in social neutering and training.

756. "Cabbages & Condoms" is a chain of restaurants in Bangkok, Thailand, with condom-themed decoration. There, instead of offering you an after dinner mint, you get a condom on the way out.

757. A man named Gay Balfour, from Cortez, Colorado, built the "Dog Gone Vacuum Truck." It's used to suck prairie dogs out of their burrows.

758. Conservationists in South Africa are infusing a special red dye into the horns of live rhinos. The mixture renders the horn completely useless to poachers that are trying to sell it commercially and also has a toxin making it dangerous for human consumption.

759. A British man named Luke Irwin found an amazing discovery buried under his newly-purchased property. While an electrician that he hired was drilling into the ground, he hit a layer of intricate red, white, and blue mosaic tile. It turned out that the house was built on one of the largest and best-preserved Roman villas ever found in Great Britain.

760. As of 2020, there are twenty three countries that don't have any military. Some of these countries include the Vatican, Iceland, and Costa Rica.

761. Napoleon Bonaparte, the Emperor of the French in 1804, was buried without his penis as it was cut off during autopsy and given to a priest.

762. The largest jackpot payout in an online slot machine game according to the Guinness World Records was over $20 million. It was won on October 6, 2015, by Jon Heywood in Cardiff, UK, playing micro gaming's Mega Moolah on Betway's website.

763. One of the rare subspecies of pandas that only exists in the remote Qinling Mountains, in western China, is the quirky brown panda.

764. There is a tradition among the indigenous Sami people of Norway of castrating reindeer using their own teeth.

765. In 2010, a study done by the Department of Experimental Psychology at the University of Bristol revealed that under stress, caffeine makes men less, but women more effective as partners.

766. Criminal Billy Milligan had a mind so disturbed that it fractured into twenty four different personalities. For each personality, his speech pattern and accents were different, and he even sat in different ways in chairs.

767. Since 1979, no one has been reported to die from a confirmed spider bite in Australia. Deaths by spiders actually occur more when you are surprised by them e.g. when you are driving.

768. Steven Tyler, the lead singer of Aerosmith, started Janie's Fund to support programs offered at youth villages to help girls overcome deep trauma of abuse and neglect. It was named after his song "Janie's Got a Gun."

769. Mary Josephine Fitzgerald was the grandmother of John F. Kennedy who not only outlived John, but was never told about his assassination.

770. During a spring training game between the Arizona Diamondbacks and San Francisco Giants on March 24, 2001, pitcher Randy Johnson hit a pigeon while pitching, resulting in the bird exploding in the air.

771. Oymyakon, in Russia, is considered the coldest village of the world. In January, the average temperature there is 123 Fahrenheit (minus fifty one degrees Celsius), while the lowest temperature ever

recorded was 159 Fahrenheit (minus seventy one degrees Celsius) in February.

772. Elvis Presley had a great love of animals. He had a chimpanzee named Scatter among countless other pets over the course of his life, including dogs, horses, birds, and more.

773. Before becoming an actor, Chris Pratt worked as a waiter at the Bubba Gump Shrimp Company in Hawaii. While working there, he was discovered by actress and director Rae Dawn Chong.

774. The longest recorded flight of a chicken is thirteen seconds.

775. Prior to getting married, Amish men are actually clean shaven, however, they are required to grow their beards after marriage. All other aspects of Amish life are determined by a list of written and oral rules known as Ordnung, which outlines the essentials of the Amish faith and helps to define what it means to be Amish.

776. The longest living vertebrate known on Earth is the Greenland shark. It's estimated that they can live 400 years.

777. "Bib-Label Lithiated Lemon-Lime Soda" was originally the name given to 7 Up. The drink was invented in 1929 by Charles Leiper Grigg. One of its main ingredients was lithia, a naturally occurring substance found in minute quantities of bubbling waters fed by underground springs. Lithia is better known as lithium, a drug used to even out mood swings.

778. There is a cat named Artful Dodger in Brigeport, UK, that takes the bus by himself on a regular basis to travel ten miles to the neighboring town. The driver already knows what stop to let the cat off at and even brings tins of cat food for him.

779. In an attempt to convince Robin Williams to agree to voice the role of the genie in Disney's Aladdin, the filmmakers produced animated clips of the character saying lines from the comedian's standup performances.

780. Oysters make pearls as a way to relieve pain. When a grain of sand or debris gets stuck in their bodies, they ease the pain and irritation by

coating it with multiple layers of nacre, a mineral that lines the inside of their shells; hence, a pearl begins to form.

781. When creating the light bulb, Thomas Edison had a thousand unsuccessful attempts. When a reporter asked him: How does it feel to fail 1,000 times? Edison replied: "the light bulb was an invention with 1,000 steps."

782. In Dominica there is a boiling lake that is so hot that the center's temperature has never been determined.

783. Beatles' singer Roy Orbison had pretty bad eyesight and needed thick glasses. During his 1963 tour with the band, he forgot his glasses on a plane before a show, which forced him to wear his ugly prescription sunglasses that night. The look, however, ended up becoming his trademark.

784. There is a pod of bottlenose dolphins in Laguna, Brazil, that have been helping the fishermen there since 1846. The dolphins herd the fish towards the shore and then let the fishermen know when to cast their nets by signalling to them.

785. Utah reduced the state's homelessness in 2005 by 78% by providing homeless people apartments and social workers, which cost them less money than yearly ER visits and jail stays.

786. At Wimbledon championship, players are only allowed to wear all white. This dress code dates back to the 1800's when it was frowned upon and considered inappropriate to have visible sweat stains.

787. Breast milk contains immunoglobulins, substances produced by the body's immune system which work like a natural laxative. That is why breastfed babies poop more than formula fed babies.

788. Sir Patrick Stewart, the actor that plays Professor X in the X Men series, began losing his hair at the age of eighteen. He thought that no woman would ever be interested in him again. He's now married happily to his third wife.

789. There was a medieval belief that crocodiles shed tears of sadness while they killed and consumed their prey. From this myth, which dates

back as far as the 14th century, the term "crocodile tears" actually derived. The belief started from a book called "The Travels of Sir John Mandeville" and later on, it was found in the works of Shakespeare. From there, crocodile tears became an idiom as early as the 16th century.

790. In 1784, Thomas Jefferson proposed to end slavery in all the territories, but his bill was lost in Congress by a single vote.

791. The first ever character to fart in a Disney movie was Pumbaa.

792. There is only one McDonald's in the US as of last year that still serves pizza which is located in Orlando, Florida.

793. It was discovered that people are most likely to discover a good idea when they're doing a monotonous task such as showering, driving, or exercising. This is due to the fact that the body is in a more relaxed and less distracted state, allowing dopamine to flow through the body, triggering thoughts.

794. The oldest tree known to have been planted by humans is 2,300 years old according to the Guinness World Records. It's known as the sacred fig, or Bow Tree, and was planted in Sri Lanka in 288 B.C.

795. Scott Bobeck, a vertebrate ecologist at Dickinson College in Pennsylvania, demonstrated in a study that boa constrictors don't suffocate their prey; instead, they cut off their blood supply. When boas tighten their body around the prey, they actually put pressure on the victim's circulatory system, causing their arterial pressures to drop, their venous pressures then increase, and their blood vessels close.

796. Caromont Farms in Esmont, Virginia, once posted a message on its Facebook page asking for volunteers to snuggle with baby goats. The sign up list filled up immediately.

797. A professor of nutrition at Kansas State University acted as a human guinea pig for his students to prove that counting calories is the only thing that matters when losing weight. He ate junk food such as Oreos, Doritos, Twinkies, and other unhealthy snacks for two months straight and still lost twenty seven pounds.

798. Large dogs tend to age faster and die younger than small dogs. The reason why is still unclear by scientists.

799. Canadian optometrist Dr. Garth Webb invented a new contact lens that can improve human vision beyond 20/20. The bionic lens replaces the natural lens of the eye in an eight minute procedure which is also painless. It takes effect in only ten seconds and enhances eyesight for life.

800. All snowflakes being identical is actually a myth. There are only thirty five different shapes a snowflake falls.

801. Fan-made short Lego films were incorporated into the Lego movie plot. You can see them in the scene where the citizens discover their creativity.

802. Golden eagles have been trained by the French military to destroy terrorist drones so that they don't have to shoot them down.

803. Coal mine fires can burn for decades or even centuries. There are actually thousands of these fires across the world.

804. Around Christmas time, some cities spray their trees with fox urine as a way to punish tree thieves who cut down trees illegally. The urine freezes on them and is completely odorless outdoors, but if brought indoors, would stink up your whole house.

805. Approximately forty six million turkeys are eaten every Thanksgiving in the United States.

806. Based on New England Journal of Medicine reports, there is a thirty year old man from India who developed an unusual flower-shaped cataract with ten petals after sustaining a concussion from a bike accident.

807. In 2016, Jackie Chan won an honorary Oscar, becoming the first Chinese actor in history to receive the award.

808. NASA's Internet speed is ninety one gigabits per second, around 13,000 times faster than the average Internet speed in the United States, which is about 6.6 megabits per second. This is because they operate on what's called a shadow network; it's like the Internet, but it only connects a few research facilities and organizations worldwide.

809. In Chongqing, China, there is a zoo called the "Lehe Ledu Wildlife Zoo" where visitors are placed in cages instead of the animals. The cages are stalked by lions and tigers, so the guests are warned to keep their fingers and hands inside the cage at all times.

810. In 2013, a dog named Killian alerted their owners about the abusive behavior of a babysitter against their baby boy. Every time the babysitter was around, he would growl and stand between the baby and the sitter. The parents later recorded the abuse and the sitter was arrested.

811. In 2012, after research was done for packaging tobacco products by the Australian government, it was determined that the color Pantone 448 C, also known as opaque couche, is the most offensive color to put beside the health warnings related with smoking. The color is used to make the cigarette packages look as unappealing as possible to discourage people from smoking.

812. The Photoshop Law is a regulation adopted by Israel in March of 2012. The law specifies that fashion and commercial models should have a body mass index (BMI) of at least 18.5. To put it into perspective, a healthy BMI is between 18.5 and 24.9.

813. The longest natural rock span in the world is found in the landscape arch in Arches National Park, Utah. It has a span of 290 feet (eighty eight meters).

814. If a person sleeps too much, sits too much, and has an overall sedentary life, they are four times more likely to die early.

815. The reason your eyes are red in some photos is because the flash of the camera passes into the eye, through the pupil, reflects the fundus at the back of the eye and appears red because of the blood in they eye.

816. A Canadian woman originally from Iraq known as Basma Hameed learned how to tattoo so she could cover the burn scars she received on her face when she was a child. The results were impressive and now she runs a business that helps other burn victims by tattooing discolored scars to match their own skin tone.

817. Dolphins have two stomachs, one for storing food, and the other for digesting it.

818. Barcelona Football Club has a sponsorship deal with UNICEF where it actually donates one and a half million euros a year while wearing its logo.

819. The ten documented people who have lived the longest are all women, ranging from 116 years old to 122 years old.

820. The "Oombrella" is a smart connected umbrella that can predict when it's about to rain and send a notification to your smartphone reminding you to bring your umbrella along. If you happen to forget it in a place, it can send you a notification via Bluetooth that you forgot it before you get too far.

821. In 2015, a French couple named their baby "Nutella." A judge ruled that it was contrary to the child's best interest to bear that name, as it was the name of a spread. The parents failed to appear in court, and they renamed the child Ella.

822. Echidnas have a four headed penis. Also known also as spiny anteaters, they actually don't use their penis to urinate and it only leaves the body during an erection.

823. Reindeer's antlers in Finland are sprayed with a reflective paint by herders so that they won't cause as many traffic accidents.

824. In 2013, a research conducted by the Oxford University showed that guys need to have at least two "boys night" a week to stay healthy.

825. Instead of having a mouth, the common housefly has an eating tube through which it vomits a drop of fluid from its stomach onto its meal that dissolves the nutrients. It then sucks up the fluid along with the nutrients, leaving behind a great amount of germs.

826. The identity of the unknown wizard at the back of "Harry Potter and the Philosopher's Stone" first edition generated a lot of debate when the book was first released. Thomas Taylor, the illustrator, later revealed he based it on his father after being told to draw a wizard to decorate the back cover.

827. In the Judaism religion, there are eight different levels of charity. The highest level being supporting someone into finding them a job which allows them to be self-sufficient.

828. There is an annual beauty pageant held in the village of Ramygala, Lithuania, where the contestants are goats. Nearly 500 people attend the parade in honor of the goats, a traditional symbol of the northern village.

829. After death, rigor mortis (postmortem rigidity) sets in within two to six hours from the hour of the death, starting with the eyelids, neck, and then jaw.

830. Pre 2006, all cosmonauts in Russia carried machetes, pistols, and shotguns into space so when they returned they were able to defend themselves in the Siberian wilderness against bears, wolves and other animals.

831. "Oliosponge" is a reusable sponge developed by scientists that can absorb oil from the surface of water as well as below the surface. The sponge can help improve the ability to clean up large oil spills, as not all of the oil sits on the surface.

832. On August 1, 1981, MTV played on air the first ever video, which was "Video Killed the Radio Star" by the Buggles. The very first original broadcast is available on YouTube.

833. A study led by Doctor Ronelle Welton from the University of Melbourne concluded that, between 2000 and 2013, horses caused more deaths than poisonous snakes and insects. Horses were actually responsible for seventy four deaths; bees and stinging insects caused twenty seven; snakes also caused twenty seven deaths; and spiders actually killed no one.

834. The reason why bruises turn colors is because the body is breaking down and reabsorbing the hemoglobin that leaked from the broken blood vessels.

835. In the past, the toga was only allowed to be worn by free Roman citizens. Foreigners and exiled citizens could not appear in public wearing one.

836. A gigapixel art camera for preserving paintings has been created by the Google Cultural Institute. The device can scan a three foot by three foot (0.9 meter by 0.9 meter) painting in complete detail in thirty minutes, while other devices used to take a full day.

837. The only planet that rotates on its side is Uranus. Its spin axis lies ninety eight degrees off its orbital plane with the sun. If compared to other planets, no other is tilted more than thirty degrees off its axis.

838. Before legendary actor Christopher Walken started his acting career, he worked as a circus owner's apprentice. During shows, he acted as the lion tamer performing alongside a lioness named Sheba.

839. The largest volcano and mountain in the solar system is actually Olympus Mons, located on Mars. It's over sixteen miles (twenty five kilometers) high, making it three times the height of Mount Everest.

840. Red Bull grew so much in 2019 that they almost sold as many cans of its drink than people on the planet. They sold 7.5 billion cans and the world population is 7.8 billion.

841. According to Tom Grazulis, a tornado specialist, about 75% of all tornadoes happen within the United States.

842. The national animal of Brazil is the jaguar, also known as "Panthera Onca," its scientific name. It is the largest carnivorous mammal in Central and South America and it can weigh up to 211 pounds (ninety five kilograms).

843. Papyrophobia is the fear of dry paper. Actress Megan Fox suffers from it.

844. Hitler actually had a pet alligator named Saturn that the Russians were gifted by the British government.

845. If a cat looks at you straight in the eyes and blinks slowly, it's actually trying to tell you that it's in love with you.

846. If one day you find a stranded dolphin, do not help it to get back into the water. Dolphins sometimes beach themselves purposely because they are sick or injured, beaching themselves to avoid drowning.

847. Okapi is a mammal that has stripes like a zebra and a body of a horse, although it's closely related to the giraffe, not the zebra or horse. Its stripes help break up its body outline, making it hard to find. In fact, the species was so hard to find that Western scientists didn't know about it until 1901.

848. Inventor Thomas Edison once tried to invent a "spirit phone" to contact the dead in the 1920's. Although most people thought he was joking, he genuinely wanted to create an ethereal device that would summon to the living voices of the dead and record them for posterity.

849. The Airlander 10 is the largest airship of the world, measuring ninety two meters (301.7 feet) long. It's filled with almost 1,300,000 cubic feet (37,000 cubic meters) of helium and can reach an altitude of 2.9 miles (4.8 kilometers). The airship has been nicknamed as the flying bum and it can remain in the sky for up to five days.

850. Master builder at LEGO, Steve Gerling, had never touched a single LEGO before he started his job.

851. Although the Darwin's bark spider is small and non-poisonous, it can spin a web sixty five feet (twenty meters) across that is able to span an entire river and it's stronger than Kevlar.

852. There are therapists known as wealth therapists who help super wealthy individuals who are mentally unable to cope with their wealth.

853. When actress Charlize Theron was fifteen years old, her mother shot and killed her alcoholic father in self-defense.

854. The largest plane in the Air Force is the Lockheed Martin C-5. It's large enough to transport entire submarines.

855. "Puggle" is the name given to a baby echidna or platypus.

856. Peter Skyllberg survived for over two months when his car was snowed in by staying warm in a sleeping bag and eating the snow.

857. The sorcerer's name in Disney's "Fantasia" is Yen Sid; the name is actually Disney spelt backwards. This is because Walt Disney himself was a great inspiration for the character.

858. Zalipie is a village in southeastern Poland where all the cottages are painted with floral designs. Over a hundred years ago, women used to paint over the dark spots of soot that were caused by their fires with paintings of flowers, and the tradition continues to this day.

859. Based on a Gallup poll, New Hampshire is the least religious state in the United States as of February, 2016. The poll showed that only 20% of people in New Hampshire are actually religious.

860. The distance between the surface and the center of the Earth is about 3,960 miles (6,378 kilometers) according to Universe Today.

861. Lycanthrope is a condition where sufferers have delusions where they think they are a wolf or another wild animal.

862. "Hangover Helpers" is a company that, for $20 a person, makes your hangover go easy. They will bring you Gatorade, cook you a home-made burrito for breakfast, clean the room that your party was held in, and do all the dirty dishes.

863. Maria and Lucy Aylmer are some of the few, world's only non-identical, mixed race twins. One takes after their mother with a darker skin complexion while the other has a fairer skin complexion like her father.

864. A clock that runs for 10,000 years was built by the Long Now Foundation to be placed in a West Texas cave. The clock measures time in centuries and millennia, instead of minutes and seconds. It has a century hand and has a cuckoo that will sound every thousand years at each new millennium. It's also programmed to chime periodically, with each chime sound being unique and never repeated.

865. Animal abuse is now being tracked by the FBI the same way they track homicides and assaults. The logic behind it is that if you abuse animals, there is a good chance that you would do the same to a person, so they have classified animal cruelty as a group A felony.

866. Between 2003 and 2005, Philip Eckmans, a Belgian who was living in Spain, developed a new sport called "Bossaball." The game combines the elements of volleyball, football, and gymnastics with music, and is

played between two teams on an inflatable court that has a trampoline on each side of the net.

867. There are over three million lakes in the state of Alaska. In fact, 86,000 square miles (138,000 square kilometers) of Alaska is covered by water.

868. Research has shown that when men text more in a relationship, both partners are less happy and the women wants to end the relationship, however, when the woman texts more often, both parties are more fulfilled and happier in the relationship.

869. The steel shortage during the war caused the Pentagon to be so shorter than it originally was. When the structure was built, it initially had 11,700,000 cubic feet (332,000 cubic meters) of reinforced concrete, mostly taken from the grounds around the Pentagon itself.

870. The "Fat Brad the Cookbook" is a book that contains all the foods that actor Brad Pitt has eaten on screen.

871. Atmospheric rivers, or rivers in the sky, are weather systems that move high concentrations of water vapor outside the tropics and can bring strong winds and floods.

872. A study published in The Journal of Addiction in 2008 indicated that roughly 76% of adults experience some form of hangover after drinking.

873. After the movie "Finding Nemo" was released, the demand for home aquariums tripled. The demand was met by large-scale harvesting of fish from the ocean, which devastated clown fish populations.

874. Although penguins cannot fly, they can still get air born by jumping. Some smaller species of penguins can jump as high as ten feet (three meters) in the air.

875. By licking a US stamp, you consume 1/10 of a calorie. However, by licking a British stamp, you get 5.9 calories per lick, and the adhesive on a larger commemorative or special British stamp contains 14.5 calories.

876. Weather in the United States is actually affected by pollution in

China. Once the pollution gets into the atmosphere over the US, it stops clouds from producing rain and snow. It also takes just five days for the jet stream to carry heavy air pollution from China to the United States.

877. "Cover," the Dutch apparel company, has included technology in the creation of jackets and bags that block every in and outgoing signal, making the wearer completely untraceable by modern tracking devices such as computer chips embedded in credit cards. It can even take you off the cell phone grid.

878. On October 7, 1916, Georgia Tech beat Cumberland College 222-0, setting the highest scoring college football game ever.

879. Nintendo and Universal have teamed up to create new Nintendo themed areas at Universal Studios in Japan, Universal Orlando Resort, and Universal Studios Hollywood. Visitors there are able to experience what it is like to be inside their favorite video games.

880. An epizootic is the term used to refer to an outbreak of disease that affects many animals at the same time.

881. In the English language, the only four words that end with "dous" are: tremendous, horrendous, stupendous, and hazardous.

882. Montpelier, Vermont, is the only state capital in the United States without a McDonald's.

883. Pizzlies and growler bears are hybrid bears. They are the result of a cross between a polar bear and a grizzly bear. If the father is a polar bear, they are called pizzlies. If the father is a grizzly, they are called growler bears.

884. If adjusted for inflation, George Washington was worth a staggering $525 million.

885. It's possible to buy snake wine in some countries like China, Vietnam, and throughout Southeast Asia. The alcoholic drink contains a whole venomous snake in the bottle and also includes insects, herbs, and other animals.

886. There are only two fifteen letter words in the English language that do not repeat a letter: dermatoglyphics and uncopyrightable.

887. National Geographic offers expeditions to exotic places like Antarctica. Anyone who pays for it can join the trip.

888. In 1892, the Gallaudet University, an all deaf school, invented the football huddle to prevent opposing teams from seeing their sign language.

889. The loudest burp ever recorded by a male, according to the Guinness World Records, was 109.9 decibels. It was achieved by Paul Hunn on August 23, 2009, in the UK.

890. Hippopotamuses are usually vegetarians. However, several times they have been documented cannibalizing one of their own dead.

891. Chinese hair stylist Wang Xiaoyu is trained in the art of kung-fu and can actually cut hair while standing on his head.

892. Shemika Charles, the limbo queen, had been training six hours a day since she was a teenager. In 2010, she set a world record and is now so flexible that she could even limbo under a car.

893. High school student Hayden Godfrey had several jobs while in high school. He saved money for a year and a half and bought a flower for each of the 834 girls at school so no one would miss out and they could all feel joy for the day.

894. In some hospitals there exists a device that detects exactly where the patients' vein is and projects it on their skin.

895. According to the Guinness World Records, Rosa Zazel Richter was the first human to be cannonballed, back in 1877. She was shot at a distance of about twenty feet (six meters) at Westminster Aquarium in London, England.

896. According to vet doctor Joyce Armen, given the huge mass that horses have, they can safely drink alcohol.

897. Chaim Witz was originally the name of Gene Simmons from Kiss. He was born on August 25, 1949, in Haifa, Israel.

898. As far back as 200 B.C., the Han Dynasty of China drilled for natural gas, transported it in pipelines and gas containers, and burned it

on stoves, even though natural gas only became commonly used in the 1800's.

899. Simcardia is an artificial heart device that allows people to live provisionally without a heart. The device is frequently used by those who are waiting for a heart donor.

900. In 2000, the cigarette company Phillip Morris introduced fire-safe cigarettes, which actually had a higher risk of starting fires when left unattended.

901. Jack Ryan, the original creator of the Barbie Doll, used to previously design military grade missiles.

902. One of the most needed items at homeless shelters are socks, however, they are often the least donated.

903. Over twenty people die each year using elevators in the US alone. Over a thousand die from taking the stairs however.

904. In New Zealand, there is a group of caves known as "The Waitomo Caves" that were created over thousands of years by underground streams. Millions of glowworms illuminate the caves and there is a central glowworm grotto where most of the luminescent worms live.

905. According to a study published in the Journal of Neuroscience, anxiety disengages the prefrontal cortex, which is a region of the brain that plays an important role in flexible decision making.

906. Based on studies made by Australian researchers at the Commonwealth Scientific and Industrial Research Organization, drinking a cup of Asian pear juice before drinking alcohol can result in reduced hangover symptoms the very next day.

907. The Hoba meteorite is the largest meteorite and also the largest piece of iron ever found. It was discovered in Namibia by a farmer who was plowing his field, in 1920. According to estimations, the meteorite weighed sixty six tons and measured 8.9 feet (2.7 meters) long, 8.9 feet (2.7 meters) wide, and about three feet (0.9 meters) thick. Experts guess that it fell to Earth approximately 80,000 years ago.

908. It's known that dinosaurs often used to swallow big rocks, which stayed in their stomach and helped them grind up food.

909. A survey conducted in the US workforce showed that over 30% of workers would give up a raise in exchange for seeing their immediate supervisor fired.

910. Johannes Stotter is an artist that spent over four years painting a woman to resemble a parrot.

911. In 2016, Wringling Bros Barnum and Bailey Circus retired all elephants in their show. The animals went to a Florida conservation spot where they actually help with cancer research, as they have a special P53 gene known to help fight cancer.

912. According to an analysis conducted by Swift Key, Canada uses the poop emoji more than any other country in the world. In France hearts are number one, while Australia leads the world in alcohol and drug related emojis.

913. John and Frances Canning invited Queen Elizabeth to their wedding in Manchester in 2012 as a joke. They were surprised and astonished when she actually showed up.

914. Male platypuses possess venomous spurs; they can even sense electromagnetic fields just like a fish.

915. In the United States, nearly one billion birds die each year due to collisions with glass. Even though most people have seen or heard a bird hit a window, they usually think that it's an unusual event, but the statistics show the opposite.

916. Scissors were invented by Leonardo da Vinci.

917. Thompson & Morgan, a UK-based horticulture company, has developed a plant that grows both cherry tomatoes and potatoes. It was developed in Canada and it's called the ketchup and fries plant; it can be bought in Canadian Costco retailers and even in some independent garden centers.

918. On May 19, 2004, a boa constrictor got itself trapped between two huge generation units, causing a fifteen-minute nationwide blackout in

Honduras. When the boa was electrocuted, it triggered a short circuit that caused the emergency system to shut down the entire power plant.

919. To honor fallen astronauts, Apollo 15 crew placed a small aluminum sculpture on the moon as well as a plaque bearing their names. In 1971, that number was fourteen.

920. Based on studies performed by biologist Dr. Sandra Goutte of Sorbonne University in Paris, some frogs have developed ultrasonic mating calls that they can use to be heard over rushing water to find a mate.

921. In Nashville, Tennessee, there is a vending machine that dispenses real cars. It has five stories and is fully automated.

922. Susan McLeary, a floral designer based in Michigan, makes jewelry out of plants that you can wear for two to four weeks, and then you can transfer them to containers and keep them as plants.

923. Mark Zuckerberg, the creator of Facebook, spent thirty million dollars in 2013 buying four houses around him so he could have some peace and quiet.

924. In Hawaii, it is illegal to own a hamster, gerbil, or ferret. It's also forbidden to own an alligator, a piranha, or a toucan.

925. Based on existing records, it has snowed twice in the Sahara desert, once in 1979 and then in 2012.

926. According to the Journal of Meteoritics and Planetary Science, the blade on the dagger found in Tutankhamen's tomb is made with materials from a meteorite. Scientists performed different tests on the blade to deeply study the elements that composed it. It was found to contain iron, nickel, and cobalt; all materials found in chunks of space rocks.

927. Before the Apollo 11's team was set to launch, astronauts Buzz Aldrin, Neil Armstrong, and Michael Collins signed a significant number of envelopes as a form of life insurance for their families. All envelopes were given to a friend who, on important days such as the day they landed on the moon, would give an envelope to their families. In case they did not return from the moon, their families could sell them.

928. Approximately a quarter of all Russian males die before the age of fifty five, mostly due to alcoholism.

929. In 2014, the music video for Psy's Gangnam Style became the first video to surpass two billion views on YouTube, forcing them to upgrade from a thirty-two-bit integer system to a sixty-four-bit one.

930. Al Capone, also known as Scarface, was an American gangster who was known to send flowers to rival gang members' funerals. One time he even spent five thousand dollars for a single funeral.

931. The actor who voices Darth Vader, James Earl Jones, began to stutter as a child, and it got so serious that, at times, he couldn't talk to anyone but himself and close family members. When the stutter persisted in his high school years, his English teacher advised him to memorize speeches and sign up for oratorical competitions, and that's how he succeeded in curing his stutter.

932. Black panthers are not a real species. They are actually jaguars or leopards who have melanism, a condition that causes them to have black skin. It's similar to being albino but in reverse.

933. "AKA Hoverboards," a type of motorized self-balancing scooters, are actually illegal in New York City.

934. Up to twelve ounces (300 milliliters) of liquid can be held by the average human bladder.

935. While playing Pokémon Go, nineteen year old Shayla Wiggins from Riverton, Wyoming, found a dead body floating in a river. She was trying to find a Pokémon from a natural water resource, but shockingly stumbled across something else.

936. Paul Walker actually owned the blue Toyota Supra that he drives off in at the end of Fast and Furious 7.

937. Having bridesmaids in a wedding was originally intended to confuse evil spirits or those who wished harm on the bride.

938. Clara da Cruz Almeida, a South African architect, has designed a little portable house. It can be packed into a 258 square foot (twenty four square meter) pod and shipped anywhere.

939. Google actually hires camels to carry its trekker camera in order to get street view of deserts.

940. Since 2016, the giraffe is in the vulnerable category on the endangered species list for the first time ever because of years of habitat destruction and poaching.

941. In the tropical forests of Central and South America, there are eagles such as the harpy eagle that are so strong, that they hunt and kill sloths and monkeys. The female harpy eagle can actually kill prey that weighs up to twenty pounds (nine kilograms).

942. Every single restaurant that appeared on season two of Kitchen Nightmares is now closed.

943. Artist Bart Jansen together with Arjen Beltman, a radio control helicopter expert, turned Bart's dead beloved pet cat, Orville, into a remote-controlled helicopter. They named him the Orville Copter.

944. A sort of floating forest is being built in Rotterdam, in the Netherlands. A number of trees had to be removed for development, so they are placing them in boats throughout the waterfront.

945. Basketball star Shaquille O'Neal was the first of all athletes to get verified on Twitter. He also used a twitter video to announce his retirement from professional basketball way before the NBA knew he intended to retire.

946. A compound called acetaminophen, which is a common ingredient in pain relievers such as Tylenol, has been found to make people less empathetic towards others, according to research conducted in 2016 at Ohio State University. This means it reduces the users' ability to understand other people's pain.

947. When his own mobile phone rang during court proceedings in 2013, Raymond Voet, a judge from Michigan, held himself in contempt of court and imposed a twenty five dollar fine on himself. From that day, Voet has put up a notice at his courtroom stating that any attendant whose electronics disrupted proceedings would be held in contempt, and that he himself wasn't an exception.

948. At the Amherst Massachusetts campus of Hampshire College, there's a yearly Easter tradition where students go into the woods in the morning to hunt for "Easter kegs." Senior students work together to purchase beer kegs, take them into the woods, and hide them behind rocks and inside patches of dirt.

949. Nintendo started back in 1889 as a playing card maker, and its products became a hit with the Yakuza, of all people. The criminal organization ran gambling parlors, and they ordered lots of cards from Nintendo, making them their main supplier. Were it not for the vast sums of money they got from supplying the Yakuza, Nintendo might not have grown to be the big video game company we know today. In an ironic turn, after Nintendo started making their popular Super Nintendo Entertainment Systems (SNE's) and video games, the Yakuza started robbing their daytime shipments, and the company was forced to start transporting their products at night.

950. Pierce Brosnan performed in a circus for three years as a fire eater, before he became the actor who played Remington Steel and James Bond.

951. Roman emperor Gallienus discovered that a jewel dealer had sold fake gems to his wife, so he had him arrested and thrown into an empty arena. He let the man stay there nervously listening to the roaring sounds of hungry lions, waiting to be torn to pieces. When the cage doors finally opened, instead of a vicious lion, a little chicken walked out. A herald then declared that the man had practiced deceit, and in turn he had had deceit practiced on him.

952. Although ketchup can expire, the acidity of the vinegar, tomatoes, and the sugar used to make it gives it a rather long shelf life. If a can remains sealed, it can stay good for about two years past the indicated expiry date.

953. A fifteen year old Pakistani school boy named Iksas Hassan confronted a suicide bomber who was about to enter his school on January 6, 2014. The bomber was forced to detonate before he entered the school that had 2,000 students, and although Hassan was killed, he saved the lives of hundreds of kids. He was considered a

national hero in Pakistan, and was awarded a posthumous Star of Bravery.

954. Leonardo da Vinci was a genius and famous artist in his time. He was also paranoid, dyslexic, and ambidextrous. He could paint or draw forwards with a single hand, and use the other hand to write sentences backwards.

955. Dogs have a higher likelihood of answering to high-pitched voices, similar to the kind we use to talk to babies, than normal toned voices, according to the University of York researchers.

956. Ribbon worms start eating themselves when they run out of food. According to experts, they can eat up to 95% of their own bodies, and still survive, which makes them highly adaptive creatures.

957. When trains were first invented, some believed that women shouldn't travel at speeds of fifty miles (eighty kilometers) per hour or higher because it would cause their uteruses to fly out of the body.

958. Botulinum is the most lethal of all toxins known to man, but it's also the active ingredient in Botox injections, and additionally, it's used for muscle spasm treatment.

959. Dodge City, Kansas, was such a dangerous place between 1876 and 1885, that any adult living there had a one in sixty one chance of getting murdered.

960. The four largest doors on Earth are found on NASA's Vehicle Assembly Building, and they are all 456 feet (139 meters) high. It takes forty five whole minutes to open or shut the doors completely.

961. A conservation group called Oceania released a report in 2013 claiming that about one third of all fish served in sushi restaurants and sold in stores aren't really the kind the buyer thinks they are. Because of wrong labeling, you might be eating the king mackerel while thinking its white tuna.

962. The National Park Service claims that George Washington ended up with a biracial family after Parke Custis, his adopted son, had children with their slaves.

963. Because of the high number of suicides committed at Mapo Bridge in Seoul, South Korea, in 2012, the local authorities partnered with ad and insurance companies to start a campaign where paintings, sculptures, motion activated lights, and messages were put there. This was meant to show people that they weren't alone. Sadly, the next year, the rate of suicides increased six fold.

964. In 2014, "Condiment Junkie," a UK-based sensory branding company, performed an experiment where they played recordings of cold and hot water being poured into glasses, and people were asked to identify if the water was cold or hot. Amazingly, 96% of participants could identify hot and cold water from the sounds. It's because hot and cold water have differences in viscosity, which affect how the water pours, and by extension how it sounds.

965. The Great Fire of London left more than 70,000 people homeless after destroying more than 13,300 buildings in 1666. Despite all the destruction, only six deaths were verified in official records.

966. A census conducted in 2012 shows that in South Atlantic British territory of the Falkland Islands, there are only 2,932 permanent residents, but there are more than half a million sheep. This means that for every single person, there's about 167 sheep.

967. Around a billion cigarette lighters are sold in America every year, and of those, roughly 700 million are imported with 400 million of them coming from China alone.

968. Steven Spielberg and Amy Irving had a prenup in place, but when they got divorced, the judge tossed out the prenup and awarded Amy a $100 million settlement. This was mostly because the prenup was written on a cocktail napkin.

969. There's an estimated $771 trillion worth of gold in oceans across the world, but much of it is dissolved into the salty water, so it can't be extracted.

970. It's illegal to have domestic rabbits for pets in Queensland, but all other Australian states permit it. You can be fined $45,000 for violating that law.

971. In the United States, the first Copyright Infringement case to ever go on trial happened in 2009, and it involved Jamie Thomas-Rasset, a thirty two year old woman. She was found guilty of downloading twenty four songs from the web. She was fined $80,000 for every song, or $1.9 million in total.

972. Humans are the only creatures whose brains tend to shrink. The brains of chimpanzees and other animals stay the same.

973. Trains that travel along the Iron Ore Line down to the Swedish Coast generate about five times the quantity of electricity that they use up. That electricity is used to power nearby towns, as well as other trains.

974. Tires used by NASCAR race teams are pumped with nitrogen unlike regular tires which use air. It's because nitrogen expands and contracts more consistently, giving the car better handling and traction that it would have if it used regular air.

975. "Memento," the neo-noir psychological thriller movie made by Christopher Nolan, and released on September 5, 2000, is regarded by some experts in Neurology as one of the most realistic depictions of anterograde amnesia throughout the history of motion pictures.

976. The US received a birthday card from Poland in 1926, and more than five million people had signed it.

977. Otto Fredrick Rohwedder was the first person to sell sliced bread, and he did it in America in 1928, in Davenport, Iowa. In 1912, Otto invented the single loaf bread slicing machine, which was the first in the world. He marketed his invention as the single greatest advancement in the baking industry, since they started wrapping bread, and he was right, because we term great ideas these days as "the greatest thing since sliced bread."

978. The NASA-operated Cassini Spacecraft returned to Earth on April 26, 2017, after becoming the first spacecraft to travel through the narrow space between Saturn and its rings. It came around 200 miles (320 kilometers) close to the innermost visible edge of Saturn's rings, and within 1,900 miles (3,060 kilometers) of the planet's cloud tops.

979. Kidney beans contain toxins when they are still raw, and eating just four or five of them can result in symptoms that present in one to three hours. The symptoms may include abdominal pain, diarrhea, overwhelming nausea, and vomiting. The toxins become inactive when the beans are cooked.

980. Police in Athens, Greece, have the authority to strip a driver of his or her license if they think he is poorly dressed or unbathed.

981. There is a town in Normandy called Terville, which is the only one in France to never have lost one single person in the last five wars in which the country was involved. This included WWI and WWII.

982. Tom Scholz and his band "Boston" recorded their debut album "More Than A Feeling" inside his basement, and he handed the tracks to the studio, who thought they had been recorded in a professional studio. Today, the album has sold a total of seventeen million copies.

983. Roger Fisher, director of the Harvard Negotiation Project and a law professor at the same school, published a thought experiment in 1981 on The Bulletin of Atomic Science. He postulated that the nuclear launch codes should be implanted inside the chest of a willing young person, and the president would have to cut them out of the person's body before launching the nuclear weapons.

984. The Elgin Federal Prison Camp closed in 2006, but during its operations as a minimum security prison, it was said to be so comfortable and cozy that it was nicknamed "Club Fed."

985. American federal agents used sleep deprivation among other tactics to end the standoff during the fifty one day siege in Texas at the Branch Davidian Compound in Waco, in 1993. They broadcasted loud noises all night long, using speakers that were pointed towards the building. The noises included chanting, jet engine sounds, screams of rabbits being slaughtered, and popular music.

986. Our eyes can detect a candle flame from as far as 1.7 miles (2.75 kilometers).

987. Skatole is a potent smelling chemical compound that is a compo-

nent of many perfumes, and ironically, is naturally present in human feces.

988. To treat eczema outbreaks, you can apply Vaseline and then wrap the affected area with plastic wrap.

989. Drinking beer can actually make a person smarter, according to an Oregon State University study. Hops contain a chemical that has positive effects on your intellectual function. The caveat is that you would need to drink 3,530 pints of beer per day to notice the results.

990. Australians grow poppies in farms and it supplies 50% of all the legal opium used around the world to manufacture morphine and other painkillers. Poppy farmers have a hard time keeping out the wallabies which love to eat the poppies, get high, and then run around in circles.

991. Atoms at room temperature never actually touch each other in the regular sense of the word. It means that you aren't touching that seat you are on, or the floor you are standing on, you are merely floating just a little bit over those surfaces.

992. From 1969 to date, musician Willie Nelson has only used one guitar. It's an old Martin N-20 that has developed a large hole after years of use. Nelson named it after Roy Rogers' horse Trigger.

993. Michael Anderson Godwin was on death row in South Carolina, when one day in 1989, he decided to multitask by peeing and repairing his prison cell TV at the same time. He bit into a wire which was still connected to the TV, and he accidentally electrocuted himself, essentially turning his toilet into something of an electric chair, like the one that was waiting for him.

994. About 40% of all known types of insects are species of beetles.

995. Seagulls have an advantage over humans because they can drink both seawater and freshwater. They are able to separate salt from sea water, and excrete it through their nostrils.

996. Blue Jay birds have the ability to copy the cries of other birds, including that of the red-tailed hawk. This enables them to keep off

predators, or to scare away other birds so they can have a source of food all to themselves.

997. There is a Japanese tradition that dates back 400 years, where sumo wrestlers shake babies and make faces at them in an attempt to make them cry. It's claimed that crying brings good health, wards off evil spirits, and cures brain damaged babies.

998. The Ninetieth Indianapolis 500 took place on May 28, 2006, and was the first such event to only have Honda engines in the field, because Toyota and Chevrolet had pulled out of the event. For the first time ever, no engine issues were reported for an entire month.

999. The "equal" sign was invented in 1557 by Robert Recorde, a mathematician from Wales, who was tired of constantly using the phrase, "is equal to" in his work.

1000. The word mafia is not mentioned even once in the 1972 mafia classic "The Godfather," because of threats from the actual mafia. Albert Ruddy, who produced the movie, got the green light from mafia boss Joseph Colombo to make it after he and Paramount Studios agreed to remove the word entirely from the script, and to donate the money made during the premier to the hospital building fund of the Italian American Civil Rights League.

1001. Lots of Buddhist monks practiced self-mummification for centuries. They'd only consume nuts, seeds or fruits they'd gathered from nearby mountains and forests, along with water, and they'd lock themselves in small tombs that had breathing tubes and bells. If a day passed without the monk ringing the bell, the others assumed he was dead, that they'd take out the breathing tube and seal the tomb for 1,000 days so the body can mummify.

1002. The Guinness Book of World Records actually holds the record for being the one book that's most frequently stolen from public libraries.

1003. Around the year 1500 AD, Leonardo Da Vinci, made a robot whose exterior consisted of a medieval German-Italian suit of armor, and it had an inner working mechanism. It could sit down, stand up, move its arms, and raise its visor.

1004. Dragonflies have had six legs for more than 300 million years, but they are incapable of walking.

1005. Pronoia is a real phenomenon, and it's often considered to be the opposite of paranoia. Pronoia is a condition where people believe that others are conspiring without their knowledge, to do positive things for them.

1006. Teenagers who are stressed are almost immediately soothed when they hear their mother's voice, according to a 2010 study. This happens because the oxytocin, the bond-forming hormone, is released when a person recognizes that someone they love is nearby.

1007. In lots of places in Europe and the US, people celebrate "Put a Pillow on Your Fridge Day" on May 29. You merely have to place your pillow on your fridge, and it's believed that you'll get prosperity and good fortune as a result.

1008. A farm in Delaware makes mulch out of damaged, retired US paper currency notes. An estimated four tons of the cash is turned to compost each day.

1009. Otto Frank, (Anne Frank's father), Adolf Hitler, and the great fantasy writer J.R.R. Tolkien, were all soldiers who fought at the Battle of the Somme during the First World War.

1010. The expression "close but no cigar" is often used when someone fails to achieve something just by an inch. However, the phrase has its origins from the early twentieth century when people were awarded cigars for winning games at fairs, carnivals, and other recreational gatherings.

1011. When alligators and manatees come across each other as they swim in the water, the alligator usually lets the manatee pass first. Even gators that are up to twelve feet (3.7 meters) long have been seen to do this.

1012. In Coloma, a town in California, the living are outnumbered by the dead by a ratio of one to 1,000. The town has a population of only 1,600, but it's home to 1.5 million grave markers.

1013. The CUNY Economics PhD program did a study that found that since 2011, when Uber was introduced in New York City, accidents related to drunk driving reduced by 35%.

1014. The creditors who issue the most elite and exclusive credit cards make them using solid gold, and they occasionally decorate them using diamonds.

1015. According to the Mayo Clinic, 30-35% of people over age sixty five who crack their ribs end up contracting pneumonia.

1016. When in loud surroundings, people will more likely try to hear something that's whispered into their right ear over their left one, according to a 2009 study. Also, it was found that people were more likely to do what you wanted if you delivered the request into their right ear.

1017. Project Mogul was an operation conducted by the US Air Force to help detect nuclear weapons tests conducted by the Soviet Union. They mounted microphones onto high-altitude hot air balloons which were used to detect long range sound waves.

1018. The "Stuffed Animal Hospital" is a company that operates a literal hospital for stuffed animals. They offer hospital-like services, including rides in ambulances, examinations, hospital name bracelets, and they clean and repair toys to restore their "health."

1019. On the Upper East Side of New York in 1984, Todd Berenger launched a restaurant called "Twins" which was staffed by twenty nine sets of identical twins.

1020. If mother kangaroos feel that the environment around them is too harsh to bring a newborn into, they have the ability to slow the gestation of the baby. They can also tell if the baby is male or female while still carrying it.

1021. To prepare for his role as James Dean in the 2001 biographical TV film, actor James Franco, who was previously a nonsmoker, started smoking two cigarette packs a day. He also learned to play guitar, ride a motorbike, and even stayed away from friends and family so he could get into the right mindset to play the role. He won a Golden Globe for the performance, so his efforts paid off.

1022. Pygmy geckos rarely grow to a length of more than 0.95 inches (twenty four millimeters), which means that if there's a torrential downpour in the rainforest, the geckos could easily drown. Thankfully, they are able to float because they're so small and have water resistant skin.

1023. The birth control pills used by women have been found to work for female gorillas too, according to research findings. This led many to believe that we have more in common with gorillas than we initially thought.

1024. A seal discovered in a Sumerian tomb that dates back to 3000 B.C. depicts the earliest evidence of the use of drinking straws. It has an image of two guys drinking beer through what looks like primitive straws.

1025. In the same vein as the White House in Washington D.C., the Korean president resides in the Blue House, which gets its name from the roof made of about 150,000 blue tiles.

1026. Joaquin Phoenix had the last name Bottom, but after his family broke free from a cult called "The Children of God," they changed their surname to Phoenix, after the mythical bird that rose from the ashes.

1027. When Monarch butterflies experience food shortages, they can become cannibalistic, and they can eat monarch caterpillars or eggs.

1028. The "Interstate Mullet Toss" is a charity function that's hosted along the Florida-Alabama border annually, and it attracts thousands of spectators who pay money to literally throw dead fish from one state to the other one.

1029. More people around the planet learn English as a second language, compared to those who learn it as a first language.

1030. Humans yawn approximately 240,000 times throughout their lives, and a yawn lasts six seconds on average, meaning that we all spend about 400 hours of our lives yawning.

1031. The trees on Earth outnumber the stars in the Milky Way. Even though exact figures aren't known, it's estimated that there are three trillion trees on Earth, which is way more than the estimated 100 billion stars in our galaxy.

1032. The NBA logo features a silhouette of a player, which was originally inspired by a photo of Jerry West, an all-star who played for the LA Lakers between 1960 and 1974. That logo rakes in three billion dollars annually in licensing today.

1033. The Snickers Bar made by the chocolate company Mars was named after the favorite horse of the family that owned the company.

1034. A Swedish member of parliament named Erik Brandt nominated German dictator Adolf Hitler for the Nobel Prize in 1939. Ultimately, the nomination was cancelled, and a peace prize was not awarded to anyone that year.

1035. If the Apollo 11 moon landing was indeed faked by the US government as conspiracy theorists claim, it means 400,000 people would have had to participate in the cover-up.

1036. The last person to be killed during the First World War was an American soldier called Henry Gunther. He was shot dead at 10:59 a.m., just one minute before the armistice that stopped the war.

1037. Beatles member John Lennon frequently visited a Liverpool orphanage in his youth, and that was the subject of the hit song "Strawberry Fields Forever."

1038. LeBron James, the NBA superstar, turned down a $10 million sponsorship deal from Reebok at age eighteen, because he knew Adidas and Nike would come along with better offers. A short while later, Nike offered him $90 million, which he accepted.

1039. The full name of the Captain Crunch mascot is Captain Horacio Magellan Crunch, and he has a ship that is known as S.S. Guppy.

1040. When Thomas Edison developed health issues that forced him to use a wheelchair, businessman Henry Ford, who was a close friend of his, bought a wheelchair so that the two could race them in his estate. As Edison lay dying, his son Charles captured his last breath in a glass test tube, which he sealed with paraffin wax. Charles gave the test tube to Ford because he knew how dear the two were to each other. The test tube is on display in Detroit, Michigan, at the Henry Ford Museum.

1041. An officer aboard the titanic named Charles Herbert Lightoller was trapped under water when the vessel sank, but fortunately, a boiler exploded and that propelled him back to the surface. He later rescued 130 soldiers from Dunkirk during the Second World War.

1042. Mel Carnahan died in a plane crash in 2000, and three weeks later, he won the Missouri US Senate election. The post was given to his wife Jean Carnahan by Governor Roger B. Wilson, and she served a two year term.

1043. There are exactly ten people who've been named honorary Harlem Globetrotters, and they include two popes, Francis and John Paul II.

1044. Alan Rickman looks realistically terrified in the movie "Die Hard" where his character falls to his death because they dropped him earlier than he knew they would. He was to fall twenty five feet (seven meters) onto an airbag on the count of three, but was let loose on the count of one because the director wanted an authentic reaction.

1045. In Germany's Veltins Arena, there are over a hundred bars that serve beer which come from a three mile (five kilometer) pipeline that links them all. The line can deliver more than 3.7 gallons (fourteen liters) of beer in a minute, from four cooling structures deep underneath the arena.

1046. Dull, Boring, and Bland Day are annual holidays on August 9, that were jointly created by the American City of Boring in Oregon, a Scottish town called Dull, and the Australian city of Bland.

1047. An art student at Syracuse University stole a real skull from a mausoleum in 1988 to use it in a sculpting class. He was caught by police, who later found out that the skull belonged to John J. Crouse, who served as the Syracuse mayor between 1876 and 1880.

1048. When "Hey Jude" was recorded by the Beatles, Paul McCartney accidentally played the wrong piano note and he gasped "Effing hell!" which you can actually hear at the 2:56 to 2:58 mark of the song. John Lennon thought it would be hilarious if it stayed in the song buried in the background where people wouldn't hear it but they'd know it was there.

1049. The Cult Awareness Network described scientology as dangerous, ruthless, terrorist, and in response, the religion sued the network, forcing them to go bankrupt. A little later, some scientologist bought the remaining assets of the network to keep them silent.

1050. For a ten hour trip, a Boeing 747 uses 39,000 gallons (150,000 liters) of fuel on average. This means the plane needs a gallon (four liters) for every second that it's in the air.

1051. The Grandpa Gang was a group of men that committed the biggest bank robbery in the history of England. The oldest gang member was seventy nine, and the thieves ran off with more than $200 million in jewelry and cash.

1052. When you sit for longer than three hours per day, your life expectancy can reduce by up to two years. It can reduce by an additional 1.4 years if you are watching TV as you sit down.

1053. According to neuroscientists at the University of Geneva, when you nap in a hammock, you get a deeper sleep than you do when you sleep at night in your bed.

1054. Actor Dwayne Johnson has a beard in the 2014 film Hercules, which isn't really his own, but is a prosthetic made of yak hair.

1055. Stilton cheese can't be created within Stilton village because of European Union rules. Only the English counties of Derbyshire, Leicestershire, and Nottinghamshire can use that name as per the protected designation of origin, according to British government guidelines.

1056. Oxford University is such an old institution, that it existed 200 years before the Aztec Empire was formed. The school was operational in 1096 A.D., while it wasn't until 1325 A.D. that the Aztec civilization began.

1057. Although there was plenty of evidence to prove otherwise, the CEOs of the seven largest tobacco companies went before congress in 1994 and testified that nicotine was not addictive.

1058. Swans only have one partner for their whole lives. In some cases, when one swan dies, its partner dies too from a broken heart.

1059. In the northern Swedish village of Jukkasjarvi, there is a hotel that's made from ice. It was originally made in 1990, and every year, it is rebuilt using ice and snow extracted from the Torne River that passes nearby. It's usually constructed in December, and stays around until April, when it melts away. The chairs, beds, and decorations are all made of ice, and each room is unique.

1060. When the Great Pyramid of Cheops was under construction in ancient Egypt around 1580 B.C., that's when the first ever documented workers strike happened, when the workers did not get their daily ration of garlic. They were given garlic to improve their health and increase their stamina, and when their rations weren't distributed, they stopped working.

1061. The first US President, George Washington, was the only one to ever get 100% of Electoral College votes.

1062. Several prominent people married their first cousins, including Albert Einstein, Charles Darwin, the first prime minister of Canada, John A. Macdonald, and renowned author H.G. Wells.

1063. While playing Counter Strike in 2010, twenty year old Julian Berot's online character was virtually stabbed to death in a knife fight, so he spent six months tracing whoever killed his character. He discovered the man lived a few miles away, so he took a kitchen knife to his house and stabbed the guy in the chest.

1064. November 2, 2000, was the last date when all living human beings were on Earth at the same time. After that day, the International Space Station has been occupied continuously.

1065. The Corn Flakes rooster pictured on the cereal box is named Cornelius Rooster. The Leo Burnett Ad Agency, also called the Critter Agency, made Cornelius after successfully making mascots such as Frosted Flakes' Tony the Tiger, and Rice Krispies' Snap, Crackle, and Pop.

1066. In Serbia, kindergarten kids usually strip down to their undergarments, go outside, and pour extremely cold water on themselves to strengthen their immune systems.

1067. Sloths have hair that's so coarse and long, that it's a great place for algae to thrive. The algae works so well as camouflage for sloths, that some of the animals ended up reaching for their own arms thinking they were tree branches, only to fall down to their deaths.

1068. The Pancake Batfish is an actual fish that moves along the seafloor using fins that act like feet and even have elbows. It can jump around like a frog just by flapping its tail. Its long nose can trick prey into coming near its mouth by projecting a lure.

1069. During space shuttle missions, NASA makes morning wake up calls to astronauts. The call recordings are selected by friends and family of each crew member, or by the flight controllers.

1070. There are approximately one thousand different species of bats, and they are spread all over the world, except for desert and Polar Regions. Bats make up about 25% of all mammals on the planet.

1071. When doctors in Fortaleza ran out of human and pig tissue used to treat burns, they started using the skin of tilapia, which is a popular kind of fish in the area. They got incredible results because tilapia have more collagen than human tissue, and collagen is needed to form scars. There are ongoing clinical trials, and the treatment could be used in other countries in the future.

1072. When people die in long-term space missions or in space settlements, NASA has a plan for disposing their bodies. The body is frozen in an airlock, and then a robotic arm shakes it vigorously, until it crumbles into small pieces and becomes space dust.

1073. A German shepherd called Gunther IV became the richest animal on Earth after he inherited $300 million from his dad, Gunther III, who originally inherited the fortune in 1992 from Carlotta Leibenstein, a German Countess.

1074. "L'appel du vide," or the call to void, refers to the urge to jump, or the feeling of being pulled that you get when you are standing at a high place.

1075. A report by the independent Berkeley Earth Science Research Group indicates that in Delhi, India, the quality of air was so poor at one point, that merely breathing the air in the city was as harmful as smoking forty four cigarettes every day. On one specific day, the US Embassy Air Quality Index recorded an air quality reading of 1,000 marks. To put that into perspective, anything more than twenty five marks is unsafe according to the World Health Organization.

1076. The renowned author of fantastical horror stories H.P. Lovecraft wrote a whole essay at one point, elaborating on his belief that cats were better than dogs.

1077. Fifty five year old Scott Entsminger was a Cleveland Browns super fan, and prior to his death on July 4, 2013, he asked if six members of the team could be his pallbearers, because he wanted the Cleveland Browns to let him down one final time.

1078. More than two million people showed up for French writer Victor Hugo's funeral in Paris, starting from the Arc de Triomphe onwards to his burial site at the Pantheon. He rests in the same Pantheon crypt as Emily Zola and Alexandre Dumas, and most major cities and towns in France have a street named after him.

1079. If you have to start a fire, you can use Dorito chips as kindling. The seasonings on spicier varieties and the oils enable the fire to keep burning longer. Cheetohs and Fritos also work quite well as kindling.

1080. There are biodegradable caskets known as "Capsula Mundi" – which is Latin for "World's Capsule" – that were designed by Italian inventors Anna Citelli and Raoul Bretzel. They are egg-shaped caskets that break down to form soil nutrients for a tree that can be planted on the grave.

1081. Twice as many people died of disease in the American Civil War than they did as a result of fighting. Acute diarrhea was one of the biggest problems the soldiers had. It was such a serious issue that they had an unwritten rule that said that soldiers shouldn't fire on or kill enemy combatants while they were answering nature's call.

1082. When you eat oysters, they are usually still alive. Since they go bad relatively quickly, they are served while still living so that they stay as fresh as possible.

1083. The "Bukken Bruse" flew from Oslo, Norway, enroute to the city of Hommelvik in the same country, on October 2, 1948. Bertrand Russel, a seventy six year old philosopher, upon boarding the aircraft, asked to be seated in the smoking section, saying that "if I cannot smoke, I should die." As the plane landed, the pilot lost control, and it crashed, killing nineteen people who were all sitting in the non-smoking section.

1084. According to records, John Joseph Merlin is the first person credited with inventing roller skates in London in the 1760's. He, however, wasn't a good skater. He reportedly went to a masquerade party in London at Carlyle House while wearing new skates, and he got seriously injured after crashing into a big mirror at the party.

1085. The space between New York City in the United States and London in the United Kingdom increases by 0.98 inches (2.5 centimeters) every year, according to National Geographic. The cities are essentially drifting apart.

1086. Actor John Ridder showed his testicles on camera by accident in "The Charming Stranger," an episode of Three's Company. The sitcom episode first aired on December 20, 1983, and it ran on TV for seventeen years, until a Nickelodeon viewer raised an alarm in 2001.

1087. Buddy Holly and the Crickets played at the Apollo Theater in Harlem, New York, becoming the first white band to ever play at the venue. The guy who booked the band thought they were an African-American R&B group called "The Crickets," but they turned out to be three white guys from Texas. When they discovered the error, it was too late to change things up, so Buddy Holly and his band took the stage to a rocky start, but they finally won over the audience.

1088. Joao Pereira de Souza, a seventy one year old retired fisherman was in his home off the coast of Rio de Janeiro in 2011, when he saw a South American penguin stranded on a beach, and saved it. Each year since then, the same penguin, now named Dindim, travels thousands of miles to hang out with Joao for several months, before going back to his colony.

1089. In 2017, Adam Rolston and his friend and caddie, Ron Rutland, played the longest hole of golf in history. They teed off on June 29, on the Western end of Mongolia, and travelled across the country, covering 1,249 miles (2,000 kilometers), hitting a golf ball all the way. They arrived at their destination in Ulan Bator, Mongolia's capital city, eighty two days later, thus completing their course. Rolston shot a 20,093, although it was estimated to be a par 14,000.

1090. Roger Ebert, a film critic, was the co-writer of a film called "Up," a movie about a murder mystery that involved a caricature version of Adolph Hitler, who lived in Northern California.

1091. During World War I, invisible ink was made using semen because the common techniques of detection didn't cause it to react.

1092. Traditionally, sailors whose wives deliver children when they are at sea are supposed to be the first to get off the ship when it docks.

1093. Officers in Quebec arrested four men in 2012 for robbing a warehouse and attempting to steal six million pounds of maple syrup worth eighteen million dollars.

1094. According to a 2011 report in the Journal of Evolutionary Psychology, women's voices increase in pitch when they talk to a man they find attractive.

1095. The singer Eric Clapton who he thought was his mother when he was young, turned out to be his grandmother, and his sister turned out to be his real mother. His mother had him when she was sixteen and single, so his grandparents raised him as their own child.

1096. Research shows that ants get self-aware when tiny blue dots are painted on their heads and then placed in front of mirrors. In a study of the twenty four adult ants that were tested, twenty three of them tried to scratch the blue dots off their heads upon looking into the mirror. A total of thirty ants were tested, and they all reacted to the mirror by feeling it with their antennas.

1097. Playboy founder and Playboy Bunny creator, the late Hugh Hefner, has an actual species of bunnies named in his honor. It's a marsh rabbit native to the Southeastern United States named Sylvilagus palustris hefneri.

1098. According to a study published by Journal of Science, between ten and 30% of the water on planet Earth predates the sun, and our bodies contain some of that water.

1099. Banana plants are not actual trees. They are herbs or hibiscus plants. Their trunks aren't made of any woody material, and instead, they consist of tightened leaves.

1100. A kitchen chopping board has about 200% more fecal bacteria on average compared to a toilet seat.

AFTERWORD

Did you enjoy the book or learn something new? It really helps out small publishers like Scott Matthews if you could leave a quick review on Amazon so others in the community can also find the book!

Printed in Poland
by Amazon Fulfillment
Poland Sp. z o.o., Wrocław

63399258R00078